'When it comes to the crunch, *Words that go Ping* is bound to reverberate. Zipping between Norwegian kisses and Japanese silence, my brain is still humming.'

David Astle, writer,
crossword maker and general word nerd

'An immensely satisfying book covering a neglected aspect of language with impeccable skill, and written in an open, flowing and humorous style.'

Susan Butler AO, inaugural editor of the
Macquarie Dictionary

'Barbara Lasserre has conjured up a magical world of word mimicry. Her wondrous little book will delight all who love language.'

Richard Walsh,
author and publisher

Author photo: Vicki Skarratt

Barbara Lasscrrc is a linguist and an aspiring jazz pianist. She has lived in France, Nigeria and Syria. After returning to Sydney she was a lecturer in language and learning at the University of Technology Sydney for over ten years.

Words That Go Ping

The ridiculously wonderful world of onomatopoeia

BARBARA LASSERRE

With illustrations by Daniel Wlodarski

ALLEN&UNWIN
SYDNEY · MELBOURNE · AUCKLAND · LONDON

Allen & Unwin
83 Alexander Street
Crows Nest NSW 2065
Australia
Phone: (61 2) 8425 0100
Email: info@allenandunwin.com
Web: www.allenandunwin.com

 A catalogue record for this
book is available from the
National Library of Australia

ISBN 978 1 76063 219 9

Case design by Kirby Armstrong
Endpaper illustrations by Daniel Wlodarski
Internal illustrations by Daniel Wlodarski
Internal design by Bookhouse, Sydney
Set in 12/17.5 pt Arno Pro by Bookhouse, Sydney
Printed and bound in Australia by Griffin Press

10 9 8 7 6 5 4 3 2 1

 The paper in this book is FSC® certified.
FSC® promotes environmentally responsible,
socially beneficial and economically viable
management of the world's forests.

MIX
Paper from
responsible sources
FSC® C009448

To Emile, a true wordsmith

Contents

1

Aargh, miaow, ker-ching

Means like it sounds

It started when I was playing Scrabble in France many years ago. My French opponent, very pleased with himself, placed the word *han*. Not a French word I'd heard of, and moreover French words starting with a strong breathy *h* are rare. I said, 'Huh?'

Then he said, 'You know, the *han* a woodchopper makes when he brings the axe down.' Aha! I wouldn't have been so confused if the word had been used in context, in the woods, or with the relevant image in a comic strip or animation—then all would have become clear. That set me to wondering about words—like *han*—that mimic sounds directly. Are they always part of an established language system and, if so, how free are we to use or interpret them, or indeed to invent our own? Are there commonalities across various languages? These questions set me off on a track that led through a thicket of inquiry and included how these words come about, the thorny problems involved in translating them from one language to another, and the inherent issues of cultural differences and taboos. But above all, in looking for answers to questions like these, I found that there is a great deal of fun to be had with word mimicry, especially when you are free to invent your own.

In the following example, from the written account of debate in the Australian parliament (as noted in the *Sydney Morning Herald*), the Hansard reporter did just that—she invented her own:

> One Nation senator Malcolm Roberts, accusing the Labor Party of catastrophising on the subject of the government's proposed industrial reforms, enriched his Chicken Little metaphor with some actual chicken noises and pecked his microphone, which performance was valiantly recorded in Hansard thus: 'bwok bwok bekerk!'

As demonstrated here, to describe what Senator Roberts did, you could use a verb (he *pecked*) or you could mimic and record that sound (*bwok bwok bekerk*). Both *pecked* and *bwok bwok bekerk* are instances of **onomatopoeia**. The term originates from Greek, from *onoma, onomat-* ('name') plus *-poios* ('making', from *poiein* 'to make'). It simply refers to a word that imitates the sound being made—as we perceive it—of the object or action that it refers to. You could describe onomatopoeic words as 'mimic words'. They are part of languages all around the globe but they are especially recognisable as words that represent sounds made by animals—for example, *bow wow* or *woof woof*, the sounds a dog supposedly makes 'in English'. We once used to put such 'sound' words in inverted commas—for example, we would write about a thing that went 'ping'. Now we tend to use italics instead, but these written signals are simply telling us that it's an onomatopoeic word.

If we compare 'a thing that goes *ping*' with 'a thing that goes fast', we can see that *fast* is operating differently, because it intensifies the verb 'goes'. You can say 'it goes' or 'it says' and follow these words with a mimic word— for example, you can say 'it went *bang*', but you can't say 'it went shriek'. 'To shriek' is limited to being a verb and has grammatical inflections, such as tenses (for example, past tense: 'he shrieked'). The linguistic term for this is lexification. (The lexicon is all the units in a language that have meaning, and this includes prefixes and suffixes such as *un* or *ful*.) The lexification of a word unit means having meaningful bits added to it so that it fits the grammar patterns of the established language. For instance, these bits can include adding *ed* to the end of a word to show that it was an action that happened in the past.

Some words are so versatile they can have a grammatical label—such as verb, noun or adverb—and also function as a mimic or an exclamation word when needed. Thus 'he

banged [verb] on the table', 'you get more **bang** [noun] for your buck', and so on, but we can also say 'the motor went *bang* when we started it'. A word like *bang* has a sensory onomatopoeic element, because it resembles the sound it describes, and it is also an integral part of a proposition, where you are telling me what happened. Ultimately it depends grammatically on the presence of the verb 'went' to make sense, and it can be described as a complement to that verb. On its own it's simply an onomatopoeic word, and sometimes classed as an exclamation. Bang!

We imitate animal sounds from an early age. A cat says *miaow* and the sound imitation has become a verb: 'the cat *miaowed*'. However, although a dog says (or goes) *woof woof*, we don't normally say it *woofed*. We say it *barked*. (The history of language can give an account of how this came about.) The word *go* is sometimes used with sounds other than those made by living creatures, as in 'the balloon **went** *pop*'. Here the exhaled air and the movement of the lips seem to be a natural way to represent the sound of air escaping. But what about other languages, such as Arabic, which don't pronounce *p* with a burst of air as English speakers do—how do they express that sound? Are they hearing what we are hearing? It's *farqa'a* in Arabic—no *p* sound at all—but nonetheless to Arabic speakers this word represents the sound of a balloon popping.

In talking about how languages are written we refer to consonants and vowels. Now here's a brief 'technical' explanation of some of the terms linguists use when they talk about consonants. This is the realm of **phonetics**—of sounds—not necessarily of spelling. Basically, linguists describe the sounds we make in terms of where and how those sounds are produced. For example, when we block the airstream from the mouth then release it with a burst of air, we get types of consonants that are called **stops**. This category includes **plosives** such as *p*, *t*, *k* and *b*, *d*, *g*. *P*, *t* and *k* are called **voiceless** plosives. If you add your voice to a plosive consonant it becomes a voiced plosive. *B*, *d* and *g* are **voiced** plosives: the *b* in *barked* is a voiced plosive, as is the *d* in *dog*. But note that we pronounce the *ed* in *barked* using the **unvoiced** plosive *t*. Same thing for *popped*, where the *p* sounds are also unvoiced.

Another important group of consonants are called **fricatives**. These are produced when we narrow the passage of air and audible friction occurs. Examples of fricatives are the *f* sound in *phew*, the *z* sound in *zip* and the *h* in *hiss*. *F* when voiced becomes *v*, while *s* when voiced becomes *z*. (As an aside, I don't know why snoring is conventionally rendered in English by zzzzz—we don't produce fricatives when the mouth is wide open. It's more likely that we are producing the French *r* sound, when the back of the tongue touches the uvula, the small lobe hanging from the back of the soft palate. But our 'vocal architecture' is as varied as our genes.) A voiced *h* is called a voiced glottal fricative, rarely used in English, except maybe to clear one's throat, but common in other languages, such as Finnish. I will introduce more explanations for sound production in later chapters.

Onomatopoeia adds colour to the way we express ourselves. It is a communication tool that is playful, fun, and often seems arbitrary; but the jury is out as to what governs patterns across languages. Are there rules, for example, to explain why people go *aargh* but don't *aargh* each other? What are the cultural as well as first-language influences that shape how we approach onomatopoeia?

This area is largely neglected by linguists, who call it **iconism** or, more generally, **sound symbolism**. This roughly means ways of producing symbols through language by way of sound imitations (*ha ha*) or sound symbolism (*the 'sausage sizzle'*). Some theorists include some exclamations (*yummy!*) and interjections (*hey!*) in a category of onomatopoeia, although note that the border between exclamations and interjections is very fuzzy. Others maintain that onomatopoeia cannot be classed in a traditional grammatical way—as phrases for instance—although interjections can be sentence substitutes. This means they **express** mental states rather than describe them, and when we hear them we have to infer what the attitude or emotion of the speaker is, and often by way of their intonation—the rise and fall and tensions in the sound they make. For example, just by saying *wow* I can mean 'I am totally amazed' or 'Did he really?'. In Chapter 9 I have a closer look at interjections like *wow*! or *yuk!*

Writers and poets have loved onomatopoeic words ever since humans first began to imitate sounds from the world around them. For instance, Shakespeare gave us the song of the night owl who sings *to-whit, to-who*. Slowly norms have developed as to how we represent sounds, to the extent that comedians use them to marked effect, often by overturning them. In Spike Milligan's 'On the Ning Nang Nong', the fun is in his play with the norms and the nonsense rhymes. Teapots don't normally hang around with cows and monkeys in the countryside, nor do they make the vibrations associated with the sound *jibber*.

Ping is a high-pitched nasal sound, very hard to pin onto a tree. Unless, of course, the tree is made of metal and hit with a tuning fork.

> On the Ning Nang Nong
> Where the Cows go Bong!
> and the monkeys all say BOO!
> There's a Nong Nang Ning
> Where the trees go Ping!
> And the tea pots jibber jabber joo.

Now, you might ask, would it seem likely to a speaker of Uzbek that cows go *bong*? Probably not, because *bong* is so far removed from what our ears identify as a sound that a cow makes. Thus, for example, in Japanese cows say *mō mō* or *mau mau*; in French, *meuh*; and it's *mu* in Uzbek. In a majority of written languages, the sound a cow makes begins with *m* (exceptions include Urdu, where cows say *baeh* and Dutch, where it's *boe*). A cow that said *bong* would have to use a relatively forceful movement of the lips to begin the sound, whereas a cow's lowing always begins with what we transcribe as a closed-lip humming sound that increases in volume as the cow widens its mouth.

These sorts of examples tell us about the conventions that have arisen in various languages to represent sounds. They confirm the sounds we try to imitate are transcribed by way of sounds that we already use in our speech. Another term for this is 'first language filter'.

Spontaneous inventive mimicry, such as Senator Roberts' *bwok bwok bekerk,* is more playful and fun than conventionalised onomatopoeic terms, but it presents enormous problems for translators. The challenge, when moving from one language to another, is to retain the psychological effect intended for the audience. And one language may have words for a reality that doesn't exist in the second language, resulting in an ineffective translation. Apparently in Chinese there are fifteen onomatopoeic words that imitate laughter! In Chapter 10 I will discuss some of these testing questions for brave translators in more detail.

❧

Polish has some wonderful onomatopoeic terms that start with colourful consonants such as *z*, or consonant clusters such as *dz* or *zg*. You can't resist saying these sounds. Santa Clause's sleighbells go *dzyń*, *dzyń*, machinery screeching or grinding is *zgrzyt*, a fire crackling is *trzask*, thunder rumbling is *grzmot*, yawning is *ziew*, glass breaking is *brzdęk*, and a hen goes *gdak gdać*.

•

Comic books and graphic novels are full of onomatopoeia, and the pictures together with the words-as-sounds create a powerful impact. But how well do they translate? I began researching this by comparing French-to-English translations of five books from The Adventures of Astérix series written by René Goscinny and illustrated by Albert Uderzo.

Whether in Switzerland, Spain or Egypt, the gallant Astérix and his band of Gauls are almost continuously at war with the Romans, so the sounds most often rendered involve those made when metal shields bump into each other: *schlang* in French, or *clang* and *bong* in English. These words contain a final throaty or velar (meaning sounds made by the back of the tongue against the soft palate, or velum) nasal *ng*, which in fact occurs more commonly in English than in French (except in the vernacular of the south-east of France, such as the area around Cannes). Hitting a wooden peg in France is *poc poc*—translated into English as *bang bang*—and punching a person is *paf paf paf*, which in English is *biff biff biff* or *wham*. Being hit by someone in France elicits *aïe, ouille* or *ouap* (*ow, ouch* or *oooh* in translation). Open-mouth vowels are all the go here, but when it comes to the sound of Obélix kissing a fish we find *tchouic* (*smack*). Lots of consonants for busy lips.

So far, easy to follow. But for a speaker of English, what would *kaïkaïikaïikaïi* conjure up? Maybe a song in Japanese? In the world of Astérix it is apparently the noise a French dog makes when it is running with a saucepan tied to its tail. It's translated as *yelpyelpyelpyelp*. The word *yelp* is much more conventional than *kaïi*, the French imitation of the sound itself but, unless you encounter *kaïi* within the context of the comic strip, it is hard to 'hear' the sound. And there is no French verb *kaïer*, but in English there is *to yelp*. The words in both languages attempt to indicate pain and movement. In both cases, urgent movement is indicated by the repetition of the sounds. The sound *kaïi* has a sharp urgency to it, more so than *yelp*.

In any context, a translator needs to have a framework, such as a comic or a social situation, to relate to. French English dictionaries invariably give a translation of *han*, our woodchopper's grunt, as *harrumph* or *oof*, not very convincing in this particular case. Moreover, each translator brings to the task his or her own idiolects—that is, their own personal way of talking—and this influences how they translate such sounds. Also, sometimes pieces of essential contextual information, such as the age and gender of the person speaking, are suppressed in the target language (the language into which the translation is being made). So, for instance, an 85-year-old's version of *ouch* or *yeow* is not likely to be the same as that of an 18-year-old, who'd be more likely to say *fuuuuck*.

As we've seen with Astérix, onomatopoeia features frequently in fighting contexts. In the Batman comics, for instance, words like *kapow, thunk, whamm, zgruppp* and *zzzzwap* tell a hero's tale and have been called 'Batfight words'. *Zlopp* goes with an uppercut to the chin, and *thunk*, a kick to the chest. But we also encounter in Batman *crunch-eth* and *ow-eth*, which I frankly find puzzling. Is the former 'kind of like a crunch'? Is the latter the sound of someone recoiling from a blow?

By using newly created sounds, you can signal to others that you belong to the group-in-the-know. Thus, for example, the sound *ker-ching* in English is a relatively recent coinage, mimicking the sound of an old-fashioned cash register. It indicates that someone is getting a lot of money. But today, with cash registers (tills) obsolete, it is used ironically by some to provide a frisson of recognition—for those who are old enough to understand the reference.

In another example, a newspaper report tells the story of a newly invented phrase in Indonesia, *om telolet om*. According to the report, it is 'the onomatopoeic [phrase] for the uniquely melodic sound of the horns some intercity bus drivers in Java have installed'. The phrase became an obsession in Indonesia after a video was uploaded onto Facebook of children lustily beseeching drivers to honk their horns in Jepara, a regency in Central Java. Again, it became an in-group sign or code for the children. Slang operates in the same way, as do emoticons and text-messaging short-cuts like *LOL*.

Similarly, showing your familiarity with certain comic books can be a sign of belonging to a community of readers. We have the feeling of sharing an environment, of having the same reference points in a culture. Words such as *splat* and *kazam* are like sensory message sticks that convey states and emotions corresponding to the scenes we are looking at. This is similar to the way people used to say 'no problemo' or 'yadda yadda' to indicate they were fans of the TV shows *The Simpsons* or *Seinfeld*.

Understanding onomatopeic words like *splat* and *kazam* presents a challenge for both the hearing-impaired and their teachers. How can we help deaf people to learn to participate fully in communicating with others when so much of our understanding depends on sound symbols? Good communicators are able to infer another person's thoughts and intentions, and these come in layers, some-times using sound words like *brrr* or *ugh*. *Brrr* could mean 'please shut the window' and *ugh* could mean 'he's doing that again, typical'. Here, the communicative effects of intonation and gesture play an essential role.

How can people who are hearing-impaired or totally deaf 'hear' words like *brrr?* By reading 'she makes a noise to show she's feeling cold'? Hardly. I have always been intrigued by the captions that aim to allow hearing-impaired people to understand dialogue and other noises in movies. Unlike in comics, these captions use only 'tell' words. For example, in the 1949 spy classic *The Third Man* a chase through the sewers at the end has very little dialogue, and captions only tell of noises—for example, 'footsteps echoing', 'man shouting in German', 'whistle blowing', 'gunshots', 'footsteps approaching'. The same is true of the scary Alfred Hitchcock movies that have captions like 'grunts', 'groans', 'shudders'—no 'say' onomatopoeia. I imagine that it is a true challenge for the caption writers to interpret sounds in a way that is meaningful to everyone. And for a person who has been deaf since childhood, a transcription of words like *aargh* could be meaningless anyway.

But educators and researchers are providing some hope for hearing-impaired people who use a signed language, and are thus considered to be bilingual. Recognising this, in 2015 Amanda Everitt, a researcher in New Zealand, set up a program teaching onomatopoeia to deaf children in a classroom situation, using visually-based multisensory strategies, linking drawings to text, and sign language to text. Her results showed that students learned to bridge the gap between English and New Zealand Sign Language so that onomatopoeia became more meaningful to them. They were able to relate words such as *grrr*, *pow*, *swoosh* and *boom* to objects or situations.

The jumping-off point for my exploratory voyage into some of the quirks, myths and theories about onomatopoeia across languages and cultures began with The Adventures of Astérix, but rather than giving the reader an endless list of how different languages interpret the same sounds, this book looks at the broader questions of how onomatopoeic words function in different cultures, how we recognise them, how the physical aspects of our voices work to produce them and why they are such fun to use and invent, both in spoken form and in literature. It addresses the issues of translation and considers how changes in our cultures, especially with regard to influences from the United States, move us and shake us. *Shazam!*

2

Eek, a mouse

Be afraid

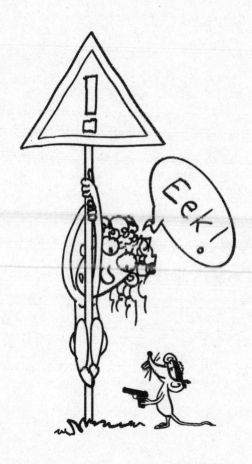

Does anybody say *eek* anymore? Why is it tradition-ally associated with a mouse? In recent times, *eek* has morphed into an emoticon for internet users, to signal surprise or distress.

In the Victorian era, the phrase was commonly used as the caption to a picture of a woman standing on a chair and screaming at the sight of a tiny mouse on the floor. The tight vowel sound was supposed to imitate the shriek of a petrified helpless female. The trope was adopted by Looney Tunes cartoons and by sitcoms in the 1930s, and used to represent a particular emotion, one that belonged only to women.

What about *eek* in, say, German? One online dictionary proposes *igitt*, which is also given for *ugh* or *yuck*, but a German speaker I spoke to suggested simply *eeeeeee*. Both versions have the vowel sound *iii* tense and tight—a pos-sible clue to the rendition of a common emotion.

Early in the twentieth century, when ladies were still regarded as delicate creatures in skirts, there was a popular myth about how to catch out a spy who was pretending to be a person of the opposite sex. If you wanted to expose an infiltrator, you threw a ball into their lap. If it was a man posing as a woman, he would instinctively bring his knees together to catch the ball; if it was a woman posing as a man she would spread her legs (to catch it in her skirt, forgetting in that moment that she was wearing men's clothes). Language can set the same trap, in terms of our instinctive responses. Imagine Hélène, a French spy who wants to pass for a native speaker in an English-speaking country. She gets her fingers stuck in a door and feels sudden pain. If her ingrained response causes her to use the wrong onomatopoeia, and she says *aïe* instead of *ouch*, it's a dead giveaway.

Culture is the way people do—and say—things. An important part of the process of feeling at ease in a new culture involves learning how other languages use particular words to reveal common physical and emotional states. Knowing how and when to employ these words and sound signals is a key aspect of communicating with others.

This chapter looks at ways in which we humans use sounds to express our fears and our suffering. There are two ways in which we do this: we use 'say' words (*eek*) or 'tell' words (she *screeched*), and sometimes a mixture of both. Over time, the meaning of both 'say' and 'tell' words can change—broadening, narrowing, borrowing or shifting their meanings, just as non-onomatopoeic words do. For example, *to croon* in the late fifteenth century meant 'to bellow or roar' and in the sixteenth century it morphed into 'to murmur or hum softly', but now it means 'to sing sentimentally into a closely held microphone'.

When we use 'say' words, we don't necessarily have an audience. So when I burn my hand on the stove, I may instinctively say 'yeow' even if there's no one else around to hear it. It expresses a release of tension for its own sake. But 'tell' words generally describe a sound we do want to communicate to others. The statement 'I *howled* with pain' assumes we are telling someone about the incident. When we use sound symbolic words, we intend to communicate to others what we are feeling, our attitude. Many of these words have become 'conventionalised'; they are now accepted currency, part of our shared vocabulary, so they have an agreed and commonly understood meaning—for example, 'he *banged* on the table' or 'I *howled* with pain'. The best way forward for us here is to bear in mind the basic difference between 'say' and 'tell' words, knowing that they can move up and down a continuum according to how and where they are used and that there are sometimes going to be overlapping areas where they can be both.

Our wannabe spy Hélène used the word *aïe* that came to her instinctively from her first language. She might also have betrayed her origins by using a conventional-ised English word like *ho-hum* in the wrong setting (for example, in a speech referring to another person's work). Putting strong stress on the wrong syllable is another trap. For example, if Hélène uses the wrong emphasis in pronouncing *gobbledy-gook* (meaning 'nonsense') and says *gobBLEdy-gook*, the hearer will not immediately register her attitude of disdain. In other words, she may fail to communicate her intended meaning.

The words we are discussing fall into the category of sound symbolism. This is a wide term that covers various ways that a sound relates to its meaning. For linguists, there are several types of sound symbolism. **Iconicity** is one of these, where the words resemble the sounds that you hear—for example, *boom*, *crash* and *squeak*. Another sub-category within sound symbolism is **mimetics**—most common in Japanese, and also Korean. Mimetic words do much the same thing as onomatopoeia except instead of just imitating a sound, they can also describe a phys-ical movement, action, or attribute. We will see how this works in Chapter 4. **Phonaesthemes** occur where clusters of letters, such as *gl*, can imply that several words are related in meaning—for example, *gleam*, *glitter* and *glow*. Phonaesthemes often relate to how we express the sensa-tions of smell, colour, shape or movement. **Ideophones** are also considered sound symbolic. These express a concept, such as weakness. They often repeat syllables and have a delightful rhythmic pattern: *namby-pamby*, *hoity-toity* and *gobbledegook* are examples of ideophones.

Eek is an iconic sound symbol because it is a tight high sound, and fear is tight and high and stretched. Think of how you would write down the shrieking sounds of some champion tennis players. It's unlikely that you would use a string of consonants such as *zzzzz* or use words beginning with, for example, *sn* or *cl*. Instead, you would be seeking to mimic the shape of the sound—its rise, fall, volume, length and pitch. Maybe *yiii-aah* could do it.

For the linguists who have dipped into the sound symbolism pond, the issue of how to class these sounds swims around the question of what makes sounds meaningful. For example, anger can be shown by words, sounds and also by loudness. In some 'say' cases, loudness is not very relevant: for example, the sound *aargh* conveys anger or frustration whether it is pronounced loudly or softly, and even when you are saying it to yourself.

The Peanuts cartoon strip, created in 1950 by American Charles M. Schulz, frequently used this word. Charlie Brown said it when Lucy took the football away from him; other members of the Peanuts gang roared it to scare others. Charlie Brown's dog Snoopy said: 'It's not the things that go "bump" in the night that scare me. It's the things that go "AAUGH".' (Note that the spellings of words like this are not fixed in concrete.)

Why does *aargh* convey anger and frustration, and why does *harrumph* convey disdain? *Aargh* came into use in the eighteenth century as a lengthened form of *ah*, to express a prolonged cry of anguish—lengthening the sound of *ah* doubled its effect. *Harrumph* appeared in the 1920s as a way of expressing complaint and disdain; its origin seems to have been the noise made in clearing the throat.

A brief detour here on the doubling of sounds to enhance dramatic effect. Linguists call this **reduplication**—the word comes from the Latin *duplicare,* meaning 'to fold or double'. (The *re-* prefix seems redundant, but that's how it is.) There are endless instances of this across all languages.

Reduplication is a feature of many pidgin languages, which are simplified versions of a melded common language that forms between native speakers of different languages who need to communicate with each other. Pidgins often double a word for emphasis—for example, *far far* meaning *very far.* In Hawaiian, *wiki* means 'fast', and there are buses called *wiki-wiki,* emphasising that the bus service is very fast. But reduplication is alive and well within most languages. In China, a young girl might be described in Mandarin as *xiǎo* (small) and her little sister could be described as *xiǎo-xiǎo* (tiny; very small). The Swahili word *choko* (poke at) takes on the meaning 'discord, trouble' when reduplicated to *chokochoko*. *Vroum vroum* is the noise of an engine revving in French, English and many other Indo-European languages (the first recorded use in English was in 1965), and in most languages the sound is reduplicated. In Indonesian it's *ngen ngen*. In these examples, the entire word is reduplicated, to vivid effect.

Some examples in English where sounds but not whole words are reduplicatd are *boohoo*, *flimflam*, *hurly-burly*, *itsy-bitsy*, and even the nursery rhyme character *Humpty Dumpty*. The words are playful, and the rhythm is an integral part of the fun.

We don't tend to reduplicate sounds when we are afraid or frustrated—one *aargh* will usually do—but when our intention is to make others afraid, repetition can be useful. British schools in the private sector traditionally have 'war cries' consisting of yells or chants that are devised to intimidate opponents at sporting matches. Typically, these involve repeated words, as in this example: *Yatte Yattah, Yatte Yattah, Yah! Yah! Yah!*

Expressing ferocity has its own range of sounds in different cultures, and war cries are a wonderful example of this. Their intention is always the same—to instil fear in the enemy and to boost morale and bonding between the soldiers—but across cultures their inventiveness is a constant. Of course, noises may be accompanied by visual messages such as posturing and displays of weapons. Think of the cries of the Native American Indians as they used to be portrayed in the classic western movies, with spears waving and war paint freshly applied. Perhaps the most famous 'Indian' battle cry comes from the Oglala Lakota. During the Great Sioux War of 1876–77, Lakota war chief Crazy Horse is said to have exhorted his warriors to fight the US Army by exclaiming '*Hokahey!*'—'Let's do it!' or 'Let's roll', 'It's a good time to die'.

During the American Civil War in the 1860s the Confederates' 'rebel yell' was intended to scare the enemy; the sound was apparently 'like a rabbit's scream' or a Native American battle cry they may have heard before the war. It was described as a long, high-pitched sound, full of pain, harsh and strident, variously rendered as *hai* or *haeow*. When a rabbit produces this sound, it is open-mouthed, its head tilted back.

Similarly, the battle cry of Roman soldiers—their *barritus*—was described by Tacitus the historian in CE 98 as being marked by a 'harsh tone and hoarse murmur'. Soldiers would 'put their shields before their mouths, in order to make the voice swell fuller and deeper as it echoes back'. The enemy would have been scared by its threatening resonance, like thunder.

Examples from other cultures are equally vivid. Today, Pakistani cinema often features what is called *kharaak* or *barrak* in Punjabi slang. It is a yelling match performed by opponents before combat, and is followed by *chingaar*, an attack shout accompanied by raised arms and the flourishing of weapons. The martial arts taekwondo and karate both have a short scream—called *ki'hap* in Korean and *kiai* in Japanese. The scream accompanies an attacking move, releases pent-up energy and is said by some practitioners to be 'powerful enough to kill'.

And think of the Maori *haka* or war cry, now performed by the New Zealand All Blacks before a rugby match. The best-known *haka*, 'Ka mate' ('It is death'), is believed to have been composed by Te Rauparaha, a warrior chief in the early 1800s. He was said to have been hiding from an enemy tribe when he pronounced these words. Te Rauparaha grew up in an environment of intertribal war; his father was captured, killed and eaten when he was a young boy, and later he became one of the most feared and respected warrior chiefs in Maori history. Integral to the message of the *haka* are a fierce posture and vigorous movements, with tongue protruding and eyes bulging, in order to fully convey the passion and defiance of the words. It is certainly more intimidating than 'Aussie Aussie Aussie, Oi Oi Oi', which itself is based on the 'Oggy Oggy Oggy' chant used by English rugby and football fans.

Now, finally, here's a question: what sound would be made by bunches of giant eagle feathers attached to the backs of saddles or to the shoulders of an armoured cavalry? Behold the Husarzy, the winged Polish warriors of the seventeenth century. As well as wearing helmets, thick steel breastplates and shoulder and arm guards, these hussars also wore 'wings'. The feathers made them look bigger, and the vibration of the feathers against each other produced a sound that has been described as a combination of whirring, whistling, clattering, rattling and hissing. It was apparently very scary. The Polish noun *syk* is the hissing sound that an angry snake or a boiling kettle makes, and *szum* is the noise of pounding waves or leaves blowing in the wind. Both words have been used to describe the noise of a Husarzy attack. But the effect would only be scary if you were on the spot; just the telling of it wouldn't scare a mouse.

3

Whoopee

The making of feel-good words

English belongs to the ancient family of Indo-European languages which are descendants of a single prehistoric language called Proto-European. This is a parent language that by 1000 BC was spoken throughout Europe and parts of south-western and southern Asia. What is significant is that in some Indo-European languages, like Sanskrit, Ancient Greek and possibly Latin, the linguistic accent was musical in nature, based on variations in pitch. One similarity between these languages is **'upness'** and **'downness'**. This is important because it relates not only to our way of seeing the world but also to onomatopoeia.

In English, sounds and words that we consider express concepts of levels of 'up' tend to be associated with happiness. 'Down' words are associated with the opposite. So we are 'uplifted' by beautiful music, and 'down in the dumps' when we are feeling blue. We talk about high culture and low culture; heaven is up, hell is down. In music, too, sounds are described as being high or low—the description relates to the frequency of the soundwaves—that is, how close to each other the sound waves occur. The distance between 'peaks' of waves is described as the sound's wavelength. Basically, the **frequency** is the number of peaks of soundwave arriving at the ear per second.

Musicians describe frequency as 'pitch'. A high-pitched sound corresponds to a high-frequency soundwave and a low-pitched sound corresponds to a low-frequency soundwave.

Larger animals have bigger resonance chambers, (throats, nasal cavity, pharynx, and so on) and the frequency of their vocal chords is low, which can make them sound more threatening, especially at louder volumes. It has the same effect as that of a subwoofer, a loudspeaker that amplifies the lowest frequencies in music.

The amplitude of a soundwave affects volume. It is a measure of the strength or intensity of the wave. It's measured as the distance from the centre line (or the still position) to the top of a crest or to the bottom of a trough of the soundwave.

The low-frequency, loud-volume war cries of the Roman soldiers as described in the previous chapter would have sounded like the growling of massed lions.

The International Phonetic Association vowel chart maps vowels according to the position of the tongue in the mouth. Vowels are classified from high to low, as well as from the front to the back. For example, *ii* sounds are front and high; *aa* sounds are back and low. Wherever the topmost part of the tongue touches another part of the mouth—the lips, teeth, hard palate or velum—is called the point of articulation of the sound we make.

Words with front vowel sounds, like *itsy-bitsy, mini, teeny-weeny* and *whee*, are associated with lightness, smallness and upness, while back sounds, as in *oomph, trump, clunky* or *Humpty Dumpty*, are associated with heaviness, largeness and downness. A *chip* sounds smaller than a *chop*. So do *slits* compared with *slots*, *chinks* compared to *chunks*, and *dints* compared to *dents*. But what can we say about *ning nang nong*? It comes under the banner of creative invention, but it follows a common pattern of high-front to low-back vowel sequence. Think of *ding-dong, flimflam, flip-flop* or *ping-pong*.

Maria Assaneo and colleagues from the University of Buenos Aires (2011) found that the 'shapes' of sound imitations expressed through vowels were more regular across languages than the consonants. What does this mean? The phonetics of your first spoken language influences how you produce sound. The 'geometry' of the mouth (the openness of the jaw, the position of the tongue, the roundedness of the lips, and so on), together with who and where we are, makes up the total effect. Compare how an English speaker would imitate the sonorous chimes of London's Big Ben clock—maybe something like *bong bong*—and compare this with the sound of a bell ringing as represented in Arabic, *tum tum*. In Japanese the sound of a doorbell is *kin-kon*, with no muscle movement around the lips.

But there are so many different kinds of bells: wooden bells, bells made to sound over large open spaces, and metallic bells to summon the maid or to hang around the necks of herd or pet animals. More differences occur in the 'tell' words than in the 'say' words such as those given above. Think, for example, about the difference between 'the bell *tinkled*' and 'the bell *tolled*'.

Early in the twentieth century, the Danish linguist Otto Jespersen grouped common theories about the origins of language into four types. The first is nicknamed the Ding-Dong theory. It speculates that speech first arose by humans echoing vibrations in nature. This theory has been put to rest along with other theories like the Bow-Wow, the Pooh-Pooh and the Yo-He-Ho theories. (And yes, these really are what they're called.) For the Bow-Wow theorists, language began as imitations of natural sounds; the Pooh-Pooh theory claimed that language began as instinctive noises and interjections that gradually acquired a meaning; and the Yo-He-Ho theory hypothesised that language originated in rhythmical grunts that accompanied physical effort. Another group of theorists embraced the Ta-Ta theory, which hypothesised that language originated from body language: wagging the tongue to say goodbye to copy the waving of the hand.

To produce speech sounds, we narrow and then open the vocal passage with a sudden or slow release. And the tension of the mouth and vocal cords and the amount of energy we expend in making those sounds make a difference to the sounds we produce. If we shriek *whee*, the mouth is stretched and tense. If we moan *woooaarr*, the vowel sound is long and the mouth is open, lips rounded, the sound coming from further back in the mouth. Try saying *whee* without making the sound, as if miming through a thick pane of glass to someone on the other side. Then do the same with *woooaarr*. When we have an *aha* moment, our mouth is open with surprise and satisfaction, while our lips are lax. It's the vowels that are running the show here.

The consonants next to the vowels are not indifferent to what's going on around them. In a word like *yippity-doo-dah*, the lips give a clue to the vowel sounds—are they rounded, spread, closed or open? And each consonant anticipates the vowel that follows. So the *d* in *doo* is pronounced with rounded lips, and in *dah* with open lips. The consonantal *y* in *yippity* is more spread-lipped compared with the *y* in *you*. Consonants can be **voiced** (requiring vibration of the vocal cords, **voiceless** (no vibration), **aspirated** (with breath) or **unaspirated** (no breath). So the *h* in *dah* is unaspirated, but in *hi ho*, for example, it is aspirated. Incidentally, there are few words in French that begin with an aspirated *h*; the French woodchopper's *han* is one of the exceptions.

In English we can use strong aspiration (breathing) to exaggerate our meaning. We can intensify consonants and consonant clusters this way. *Hoity-toity* carries a lot more disdain if we aspirate both the *h* and the *t*. And if we aspirate the *cl* and lengthen the *u* of 'hasn't a **clue**', listeners get the message that we are adamant, not vague. Compare the words *phew* and *few*. The *f* sound in *phew* can be strongly or weakly aspirated to show different degrees of relief, while we are unlikely to strongly aspirate the *f* in *few* unless we are in a situation where we need to insist that it's *few* we mean, definitely **not** *many*. These kinds of changes in the way a word is said give it 'phonic meaning'.

High vowel and consonant sounds can also be added to the end of a word to reflect a small size, or small volume, and in some cases a feeling of affection. In most Latin-based languages, as the size of the object decreases, you add a small high sound like *ita* (señorita), *illa* (casilla—little box or square on a board game) or *ette* (fillette—little girl) to the end of the word. The words for *bell* in Spanish and French are *campana* and *cloche*, respectively, while a small bell is a *campanilla* and a *clochette*.

But this does not happen in all Indo-European languages. Church bells in Polish go *gong* and little bells go *dzwon erki*, a totally different word (although based on the verb *dzwonić*—little ding). Not so straightforward!

•

In 1930 linguist John Rupert Firth identified certain sound symbolic clusters that he called phonaesthemes—think clusters of sounds with a theme. The term comes from the Greek words for sound (*phone*) and perceive (*aisthema*). As I mentioned in Chapter 2, phonaesthemes bind together groups of words that have a distinct connection between sound, or form, and meaning. For instance, in English we find a group of words starting with the cluster *sl* that are related to attack—*slam, slash, slaughter, slug*—while another group of *sl* words relates to wet substances and sliding movements: *slime, slippery, slop, slurry*.

In Australia a public education campaign called SunSmart was launched in 1981. Its aim was to encourage children and adults to protect themselves from the UV radiation in sunlight that can cause skin cancer. Its slogan was *Slip, Slop, Slap!* The message was to 'slip on a shirt, slop on sunscreen and slap on a hat'. *Slip* with its high vowel indicated an action that was quick and easy, *slop* with its short *o* associated quick movement with liquid, and *slap* with its back vowel indicated vigour. The people heard the message in the phonaesthemes and the result was some radical changes in behaviour. The Cancer Council attributed the subsequent reduction in melanoma rates to the effectiveness of the campaign.

There are many examples of phonaesthemes in English. For example, *cl* in *clang, clap, clash* (sharpness of sound); *fl* in *flicker, flow, flutter* (forms of rapid movement); *str-p* in *strap, stripe* (meaning a straight line that has some width); and *tw* in *tweak, twine, twirl, twist* and *twizzle* (going around). There is a *gr* cluster that relates to groups, greatness or increase in density, as in *aggrandisement, aggregate, agreement, grandiose* and *gravitas*, and also a different *gr* cluster relating to negative or threatening perceptions, as in *grim, gripe, groan* and *growl*. A *cl* cluster relates to a sudden noise, as in *clamour, clang, clap, clash, clatter* and *click*. Another group reflects the meaning of 'to close' or 'to fix', as in *claustrophobic, clinch, clip, closure*. One *gl* group covers stickiness, as in *agglomeration, glue* and *glutinous*, while another group refers to light, as in *gleam, glimmer, glitter* and *glow*. The *shr* of *shriek* is a phonaestheme found in a group of other words that imply 'a reduction from a normal state', as in *shred, shrink* and *shrivel*.

Some linguists argue that the grouping of phonaesthemes is superficial, and that similarities can be attributed to a common root. There are indeed many cases of counter-examples. Without entering into this discussion, let's just accept that shifts in meaning occur naturally as languages evolve over time, and borrowings from other languages allow all sorts of sounds to enter and exit, and also to take on new forms. Some phonaesthemes move across related families of languages, while some are specific to a single language. For example, *fl* is associated with movement—*flight, flip, flow*—and this is also true for Swedish, Old English, German and Icelandic, but *fj* is found only in Swedish.

Flip-flop, clippity-clop: some phonaestheme consonants such as *fl* and *cl* at the beginning of words 'borrow' some of the energy of vowels of higher frequency, such as *i*, with which they combine. So *flip-flop* has its primary energy in *flip* because the *i* has a higher frequency than the *o*. Likewise *clippity-clop* starts with a high-energy sound that signals first an up, then a down with *clop*. Repetitive *k*, *p* and *t* sounds are plosives that give us the sound of the horse's hoofs on the ground. In the 1906 poem 'The Highwayman' by Alfred Noyes, *tlot-tlot*—unlike *clippity-clop*—mimics the regularity and timbre of the hoof beats.

> *Tlot-tlot; tlot-tlot!* Had they heard it? The horse-hoofs
>   ringing clear;
> *Tlot-tlot, tlot-tlot*, in the distance? Were they deaf that
>   they did not hear?
> Down the ribbon of moonlight, over the brow of the hill,
> The highwayman came riding,
>   Riding, riding!

English is by no means the only language that inter-
prets hoof sounds with voiced and unvoiced plosives. For
example, in Arabic we find *deregin deregin*; in Turkish it's
digi-dig digi-dig; in Hungarian, *klippi-klop*; and in Russian,
tygdym-tygdym. We can hear the noise of the horse's hoofs
in these examples because we hear not only the plosives *k*
and *t* and their voiced versions *g* and *d*, but also because
the patterns, repetition and rhythms of the consonants
and vowels are working together to create the sound effect.

To *whinny* is how we describe in English a series of
high-pitched sounds a horse makes. It's *hennir* in French,
vrinsken in Danish, *řehtání* if you speak Czech, and *hinnīre*
if you speak Latin. Horses also *blow, neigh, snort, squeal*
and *snicker*, the last sound made with the mouth closed.
But the whinny is created in the horse's generous nose and
open mouth. Many languages transcribe this sound with
words that contain the letter *n*, because we produce this *n*
sound in our nose and mouth. This brings us to something
called the nasalised vowel.

A nasalised vowel is simply a vowel that goes cheek
by jowl with a nasal consonant. In other words, it is commonly found next to the consonants *m* and *n* or *ng*. When
we produce nasal sounds, air escapes through the nose (the
velum at the back of the soft palate is lowered) as well as
the mouth. Compare, for example, the words *mine* and

fit. The *i* in *mine* is surrounded by the nasal consonants *m* and *n*, so the nasal passage is open when we pronounce the vowel. The *i* in *fit* is not nasalised, but in the word *nit* the *i* is considered to be partially nasalised, and the same is true when a vowel goes just before a nasal consonant, as in *fin*. Nasal sounds are a prominent feature in the French language, such as the *on* in *Macron*, or the *an* in *vlan*, which means 'wham'. When a vowel in French is followed by the letters *m* or *n*, that vowel is called a nasal vowel; there are four types of nasal vowels, with phonetic symbols to identify each one. And it gets a lot more complicated, naturally.

European and Middle Eastern languages have nasal sounds, but what about non-European languages? The linguistics researcher André Müller tells us that there seem to be at least 500 languages with nasal speech sounds, to be found mainly in West Africa, India and South America, and to a lesser extent in Papua, South-East Asia and in Native North American languages. One type of frog in Central Nigeria is called a *nryâng* because of its exceptional ability to quickly jump—*ryâng*—when someone tries to catch it. (Think of the English *boing, boing.*) Famous British linguist David Crystal found that nasal sounds at the beginning of syllables in English were associated with pleasant meanings, as in *mellifluous* or *murmur*. For

Japanese speakers, nasal sounds add a feeling of 'touch-ableness' and warmth. For example, *node* and *dakara* both mean 'because', but *node* with its nasal sound is perceived as being more personal.

Linguists describe nasal sounds as being 'embodied', meaning that certain words may have developed from sounds produced by the nose. In brief, embodied sounds, like nasal sounds, may have gained a linguistic meaning at some early stage in human evolution, and become embedded in sound symbolic segments such as *sn*. Examples of words beginning with nasal sounds that are related to the nose or biting are *snap, snarl, sniffle, snivel, snuffle, snore, snort* and *snot*. Linguist researcher Dennis Philps shows us that these words attract other, modified words, for example, *snug . . . snaggle* (tooth) or *nose . . . schnozzle*. He also gives us examples from languages other than English. In ancient Egyptian, *śn* means to smell; in Sino-Tibetan, *sna* means to smell sweet; and in Khoisan (a group of African languages from South Africa and Namibia) *suni* means to sniff, or to inhale.

Like English, Swedish is considered a Germanic language, so we can expect to find similarities between the two. Researchers Gerd Carling and Niklas Johansson selected words in Swedish beginning with phonaesthemes such as *kl* and *pl* combined with high and low vowels—for example, *kloss* (log) and *plinga* (to ring). They charted these against physical and evaluative properties such as loudness, wetness, smell, attitude, and so on, and compared the development of these phonaesthemes with that of three other languages of Germanic origin, namely German, English and Icelandic. They found that there are often affinities between them: Swedish *klump,* (Middle Low) German *klumpe,* (Low) German *klump,* Modern English *clump.* As in English, high vowels and the voiceless consonants *p, t, k, f* and *s* combine to produce Swedish words that are associated with speed and lightness, such as *klicka* (to click) and *klirra* (to rattle, to clink). Words associated with heaviness or sliminess are created by combining low vowels with the voiced consonants *b, d, g, v* and *z*—for example, *kladda* (to mess about with), *klafsa* (to squelch), *klunka* (to gulp), *plufsig* (bloated, unkempt) and *plussig* (pudgy, swollen).

A particularity of Swedish is that putting the clusters *bj, fj, fn, gn, nj, pj, sl* or *vr* at the beginning of a word makes that word sound pejorative. Examples are *fnoskig* (silly), *fjärta* (to fart), *fnurra* (kink), *pjåkig* (shabby), *pjoller* (meaningless talk) and *pjoskig* (squeamish). (Strangely, in Icelandic, a close relative, there is no pejorative connection; it emerged in Swedish only in the eighteenth and nineteenth centuries.)

When Scandinavian and Nordic companies like IKEA or Nokia are choosing brand names they are very careful to avoid phonaesthemes with pejorative connotations. In any language, names that communicate well give consumers information about a product, such as its strength, speed, softness, hardness, weight, and so on. Studies by Gerard A. Athaide and the aptly named Richard R. Klink on the use of onomatopoeia in product names noted connections between words starting with *fl* and quick or strong movement, *kl* and a short wide form, *sp* and a long thin form, *kn* and a round form, *bl* and light, *skr* and a rough surface structure, *sk* and hardness, and *mj* and softness.

Furniture manufacturer and retailer IKEA has a huge database of Swedish names for its products, organised into a well-established system used in all its stores around the world. They include boys' names, girls' names, Norwegian place names, and so on. But their consonant clusters are always a delight. The movement cluster *fl* is used to name a trolley *Flytta* (move) and a rocking chair *Flaxig* (flapping). Their bicycle is called *Sladda* (to skid). A spice mill is called *Krossa*, which means 'to crush or grind'. Next time you're looking into your *Krabb* (choppy) mirror you can feel confident that there is a meaningful sound system in place for the names of products.

However, although the company also checks for words that may offend in other languages, a few have made it through, such as the 2004 *Fartfull* children's workbench, and the *Stenklöver* duvet set. Fortunately, they have not yet named a cushion 'Whoopee'.

4

Gahshunk

In Japanese they triple the fun

Would *thwack* or *thunk* do it in English for the noise a shark makes when bursting through a wooden door? This unlikely image with its accompanying sound is taken from a Japanese manga comic. Manga is a Japanese style of comic book and graphic novel that appeals equally to adults and children. It is typically black-and-white, featuring stylised characters with large, round eyes. The shark-door scene from the horror manga *Gyo* has become an internet meme known to all fans of this genre. Interestingly, the word *gahshunk* that accompanies the image is not a regular Japanese word. *Gashan* would normally be used to describe the noise of a crash or impact, but *gahshunk* is an example of an invented vocabulary called 'wasei-eigo'. This consists of a set of words coined in Japan and based on English words or parts of words. Linguists call them pseudo-loanwords but foreigners commonly refer to wasei-eigo as Jinglish or Japanese-English. An example is *seku hara*, meaning sexual harassment. In the case of *gahshunk* the

'Englishness' of the onomatopoeia resides in the *unk* sound, with its low *u* and final *k*. *Thunk!*

Japanese has a special relationship with onomatopoeia, and deserves a chapter on its own. There are apparently three times more onomatopoeic words in Japanese than in English, and they constitute a crucial part of the Japanese language, a natural expression of the Japanese way of seeing the world. Onomatopoeic words are grouped into four types. These are *giongo, giseigo, gitaigo* and *gijoogo*— although there is always some overlap between them—and each type has its own specific vocabulary. They are written either in *hiragana* or in *katakana*, which are two of the Japanese written language systems, the other Japanese system being *kanji*, which uses Chinese characters. When Japanese text is represented in Roman script, it is called *rōmaji*.

Giongo and *giseigo* are conventionalised words that mimic actions or sounds. *Giseigo* is in fact one type of *giongo*, which includes the imitations of all types of sounds. *Giseigo* imitates specifically human or animal sounds. In the word *giongo*, *gi* means 'similar', *on* means 'sound' and *go* means 'word'. In the word *giseigo*, *sei* means 'voice'. Linguists call *giongo* and *giseigo* **phenomimes** (phenomena + sound mimic). *Giongo* imitates sounds like rain or the noise of breaking down a door: *gashan* (crash), *sawasawa* (rustling), *zawa* (wind in the trees), *bakibiki* (impact sound). *Giseigo* includes words that mimic the voices of people and animals. The sound a cat makes is *nyanya*; a frog croaking is *kerokero*; chirping is *chuuchuu*; sneezing, *kushu*. But as well as mimicking actual sounds—animal and human—*giseigo* can mimic the manner in which someone acts or something occurs, such as *gobogobo* (gurgling), *pikapika* (shine or sparkle), *zeizei* (a wheezing sound) or *kyuru*, which my Japanese informant Hiromi tells me is the sound of a cassette tape rewinding. Other words relate to the sense of touch—for example, feeling a slimy or sticky sensation is *nurunuru* or *nebaneba*.

But it is the *gitaigo* and *gijoogo* words that are more abstract and can be most puzzling if you are learning to speak Japanese and trying to understand Japanese culture. (In the word *gitaigo*, *tai* means 'copy' or 'imitate'; in *gijoogo*, the long sound *joo* means 'feeling' or 'state of mind'.) Linguists call these words **psychomimes** (think psychology + mime). They allow us, as outsiders in a scene, to understand a person's inner state. *Gitaigo* words are written mostly in *katakana*, the Japanese writing system used mainly for 'imported' words. (These are foreign words that are converted into Japanese sounds and often abbreviated—for example, *suupaa* for supermarket.) The words often take on quite a different meaning from their English original. *Gitaigo* words are classed as a form of mimesis that depict states, conditions or manners rather than sounds, and are most commonly found in traditional texts.

According to the linguist Aleksandra Oszmianska, the fact that there is such a large number of psychomimes in Japanese reflects the fact that Japanese culture values silence as well as visual and embodied modes of communication. This means that, just as in all cultures, people communicate in ways other than through words, and that body positions and gestures are equally important for making meaning. However, in English we don't have the same type of resources within the language for communicating psychological states. As an example, *jiiin* represents the sound of staring and *shiiin* the sound of silence or of being stunned beyond words; a state of being motionless. The more the vowel is extended, the more intense the stare (*jiiiin*) or the longer the stillness (*shiiiiin*—this could possibly be interpreted as a heavy silence in English). *Hatto* is the outward appearance of tension or surprise when coming across something unexpected. The word *gutto-gūtto* means concentrating all your energy to perform an action, and can also express a change from a preceding state of mind to an emotion. By extending the *u* sound, *gūtto* expresses an action/change/emotion that is stronger and more prolonged than what came before.

Gijoogo as a concept was identified 60 years ago by the eminent Japanese linguist Haruhiko Kindaichi. *Gijoogo* words express feelings and psychological states, such as excitement and happiness, or sickness and pain. Examples are *awawa* (the sound you make when you are experiencing panic—for example, when you are afraid you are about to fall from a height), *gaaan* (shock or embarrassment) and *furafura* (the state of being dizzy—for example, the feelings associated with a hangover). A state of fun or excitement is expressed by *wakuwaku,* and a state of nervousness by *dokidoki*. If you combine these two words, you can express a state of fun and nervousness, such as when waiting for a first date—*wakuwaku dokidoki*.

Basically, onomatopoeia in Japanese calls upon concrete images to express an emotion or state of being. This is especially true for psychomimes—for example, *hiyahiya*, a cold or chilly feeling, is also the feeling of worry in a dangerous situation; and *pichipichi* connotes the sound of a small object— often a fish—bouncing or flapping, and also a spirited, active person.

❧

The *hyaaaa* feeling: I recently received a text message from a Japanese person which included an illustrative emoji, a red-cheeked face with wide eyes and hands held to each side of the face, palms out. In her message she indicated that she was feeling embarrassed, and she told me that the appropriate sound for expressing this feeling was *hyaaaa*. A similar, expanded gesture, where the arms are held out from the body with the elbows close to the waist, accompanies *awawa*, panic or feeling flustered. It's the sort of gesture English speakers might associate with pleading.

There is a lot of overlap between the four major categories. In traditional texts, such as novels, the vast majority of the sound symbolic words used are *gitaigo*, mostly used as adverbs, whereas in manga, the majority of the sound symbolic words are *giongo*, often used on their own, not as part of a sentence—for example, *ei* (shriek), *baribari* ('crackle crackle', signifying energy or electricity) and *goshi* (scrubbing, rubbing, wiping).

If you can imagine a continuum between words that imitate sounds and those that don't, psychomimes are situated in the middle. Psychomimes are vivid in a sensual way that other words are not. There is a suggestion that such sound symbolic words involve other forms of sensory perception such as smell or touch, in a similar way to how people with synaesthesia associate letters with colours (see

Chapter 5). Linguist Joshua Caldwell makes the claim that when a Japanese person hears, for example, the word *kirakira*, meaning 'glittering', they feel as if they can actually experience glittering or sparkling.

A theory on the role of synaesthesia in the origins of the Proto-European language (the lost language from which all Indo-European languages are theoretically derived) notes that, just as you point a finger away from the body to mean 'outwards', so you pout your lips (an outward motion) to say *you* in English, *tu* or *vous* in French or *thee* in Tamil. By contrast, when referring to yourself, the lips and tongue move inwards, as in English *me* and *I*, French *moi* and Tamil *naan*.

This theory does not hold for Japanese, where there is minimal muscle tension around the lips when speaking and where personal pronouns are not used as extensively as they are in many other languages. It's hard to pout when saying *anata*, the word most commonly used for 'you', or to move the tongue and lips inwards to say *watashi* (I, me).

Why are there so many onomatopoeic words in Japanese compared to English? Romanian linguist Raluca Nicolae gives us one answer by way of an illustration: to express various nuances of the basic action of walking, English has verbs such as *to dawdle, to trudge, to toddle,* et cetera, whereas in Japanese these nuances are conveyed by adding an additional word that conveys the psychological dimension—for example, by adding to the verb *aruku* (to walk) the mimetic words *noronoro* (dragging the feet heavily), *tobotobo* (sadly, dejected), *yochiyochi* (waddle like a toddler) or *yotayota* (a drunk person's walk). So 'we trudged' is *tobotobo arukimashita*—literally, 'we walked looking sad with a feeling of depression'.

More complicated still is the way the Japanese language combines mimetic words, mostly adverbs, with other parts of words. So a word like *kirameku* (to twinkle) is made from *kirakira* (sparkle) and *meku* (to have the appearance of), while 'stagger' is *yoromeku*, from *yoroyoro*, meaning 'unsteady, tottering'. *Wakuwaku* is the word for the sound of trembling—it means to get excited or nervous—and *tekateka* is how you feel when you are excited, anticipating something good, such as meeting a lover, and it is also the sound of something shiny or gleaming (similar to *kirakira*, 'sparkle', as in stars or eyes, but less 'sharp'). Together, they make *wakuteka*—the jitters. When someone is shivering with excitement and they just can't keep still, you might describe this as *wakuteka-suru*. This is an example of how verbs are created by adding the generic verb *suru* (to do) to mimetic words.

In Japanese, full or partial reduplication (repetition) of onomatopoeic words can indicate the degree or intensity of a sensation. For example, *niko* is the feeling of a smile. When you put two smiles together and get *nikoniko*, it means the whole face lights up—that's the sound that expresses the feeling of a broad grin. *Nitanita* is a smirk, a sinister grin, one that hides a secret, perhaps of an unseemly nature.

Sometimes the same stem word is repeated, as in *pak-upaku*, a mouth opening and closing. In other cases the first consonant of the first word may be voiceless, but repeated with that consonant now voiced. For example, *sama* means 'sort' or 'type', while *samazama* means 'various'. It's as if in English we might use the made-up or invented words. So, if *tum* was stomach, then *tumdum* would be stomach ache. If *picka* was choose, then *pickabicka* would mean 'carefully sort'. However, to confound students of Japanese, the voiced counterpart of *h* is *b*, and so from *hito*, 'person', we get *hitobito*, 'each person' or 'people'.

In English, if a glass is smashed we say 'the glass shattered'. But in Japanese, it's more nuanced than this. *Peshari* is the sound of something under pressure smashing or collapsing. When a word ends with *ri*, it signals that the action as a whole has taken place, and the focus is on the end condition of the object; in other words, the glass has smashed, so the whole smashing activity has ended. Another way to think of *ri* is meaning 'just once', so the event is not ongoing. *Kirari* means one little spark, a flash.

Although Japanese is not an Indo-European language, there are some limited similarities between Japanese and English sound systems as regards the high/low vowel sounds and their implications for meaning. For example, high vowels in Japanese generally denote smaller, brighter things than low vowels do, just as in English. Remember *itsy-bitsy* versus *bump*? *Isoiso* means 'moving blithely and happily', while *buyobuyo* is 'flabby'.

A further complication comes from the fact that in the Japanese alphabets of *hiragana* and *katakana*, although there are individual symbols for each of the vowels, there are no single consonants with which we are familiar, because each written symbol represents a syllable. So *k* in Japanese has to be written as *ka, ki, ku, ke* or *ko*—where in Roman script two or three letters are required to form a syllable (for example, *ka* or *shi*), in *hiragana* and *katakana* a single character does the same work to represent this sound. There is only one symbol that doesn't represent a consonant plus vowel, and that is ん, pronounced as *n*. It always comes at the end of a syllable, such as in Nihon (Japan).

Sound symbolic clusters of consonants do exist, such as *nga*, an older nasal form of *ga*, indicating hardness. It is mostly used in the nasal form in the middle of words. An example of a word that has the sound *nga*—indicating hardness in the middle of the word—is *renga* (brick), but the *ga* form can be at the beginning of words. *Ganbaru* or *ganbatte* is to stand firm and persevere. *Ganbatte* is sometimes translated as 'good luck' but luck is not implied in the Japanese term. *Chi* indicates smallness or quickness; *chibichibi* means 'a little at a time'. The sound cluster *sh* tends to represent human emotional states—for example, *kanashii* (sad) and *ureshii* (happy). The same sound cluster occurs in phenomimes such as *shitoshito*, 'to rain quietly'. The phoneme *no* indicates slowness: *noronoro* means 'moving slowly or sluggishly'.

In early Japanese the sounds *k/g* indicated 'involvement of a hard surface'; today, as in English, sounds produced in the throat and particularly using *k* or *g* still hint at harshness, sharpness and suddenness—'too muchness'. Words that start with a hard *g* sound can also describe lethargic or undesirable states—for example, *guchagucha* indicates sogginess or messiness—and *g* is often considered heavier than *k*. So *gatagata* is 'loud clattering' versus *katakata*, 'clattering'; *giragira* is too much strong light versus *kirakira*, 'sparkling, twinkle'; and *gohongohon* is the sound of a resounding repetitive cough, while *konkon* is a small repetitive dry cough. Similarly, just as the voiced *g* is heavier than the unvoiced *k*, so the voiced *z* is stronger than the unvoiced *s*: a strong wind in the woods is *zawazawa*, a weak wind is *sayasaya*. The sound of strong rain is *zaazaa*, and raining softly, as above, *shitoshito*.

What about creative onomatopoeia in poems and literature? Writers have the freedom to change the pattern of repeating syllables. The early-twentieth-century writer Kenji Miyazawa, in the picture book *Crossing the Snow*, represents the sound of children's snowshoes as they step on the hard frozen snow as *kikku, kikku, kikku*. In his story 'The Fire Stone', the sound of bellflowers ringing their morning chimes is *kan, kan, kan-kae-ko, kankokanko*—ding-dong, ding-ding-dong, ding-ding-a-dong.

Miyazawa's writing is a particularly rich source of examples of creative variations in describing wind. In addition to *sayasaya*, there are a number of onomatopoeic words in Japanese commonly used for wind—*pyupyu, byubyu, hyuhyu, hyuuu, soyosoyo* and *suusuu*. So a cold wind blowing in the north is *byuubyuu* or *pyuupyuu*. And a strong wind storming through the village is described as *doddodo dodōdo, dooōdo, dodo*; Miyazawa deliberately changes rhythm patterns for poetic effect.

Linguist and teacher Naomi Sharlin tells us that in Japanese culture, the goal of communication is not just to transmit information (as in English and other European languages) but rather to express situations so that both the speaker recounting a story and the listener interacting with the speech experience them. The importance of the manner in which something is said is significant. According to this theory, European languages are rule-governed and de-emphasise the relationship between the speaker and their perception of themselves. In Japanese, by contrast, a person has a choice of three personal pronouns to say *I*, and each one carries different messages about how that person perceives themselves in relation to others.

Translators need to be able to understand how this works in order to preserve the illusion that the essence of what is thought and spoken/written in one language can be understood in another. If you are translating from Japanese, you need to recognise sounds and movements as emotional experiences rather than simply events. For example, Sharlin refers to a famous manga where the word *shiiiin* accompanies an image of rows of students sitting silently waiting for a class to start. The English translation used 'Hmmmm', which can represent waiting or musing, but not silence.

Manga have been translated into many languages. Problems for translators often relate to how the language synchronises with the artwork, as well as the use of mimetic words. Cathy Sell tells us that commercially translated manga tend to be regarded by purists of the genre as 'foreignised'. This means the readers are well aware they are reading translations, but translations that keep references to the source culture—that is, Japan. This can include building types, behaviour habits of an age group, food types, character stereotypes, and so on. Similarly, equivalent onomatopoeic words are often incorporated into the artwork for aesthetic reasons and because the translators want to stay faithful to the original artwork/text relationship.

As Sell describes it, another trap for translators occurs when a word understood in the manga context in Japanese has a different meaning in the target language:

In *Hollow Fields* (2007–2009), a magical science series for school children written and drawn by Australian artist Madeleine Rosca, the evil school mistress's laugh is expressed as 'ohohoho' which is a common way to express a feminine haughty laugh in Japanese manga, even though in English it would ordinarily be associated with a jolly laugh such as that of Santa Claus.

Educator and linguist Hiroko Inose quotes an example of a well-translated text where the Japanese author had described a 'small private college' using the word *kojin-mari*. This is a mimetic word that describes the state of something being small, neat and organised. The translator added the word 'cosy' and in English it became a 'cosy little private college'.

If there is no corresponding onomatopoeic word, the translator can create their own word using the phonetic system of the target language, keep the Japanese word as an 'authentic' appropriated term, or simply omit the word. Some translators resort to using 'tell' words, such as *flinch*, *glare* or *stare*; or they use adjectives, adverbs or paraphrases. However, if the intention is to keep some of the source culture's colour and flavour, the last option doesn't appear to be the most effective, because it relies on the translator's personal interpretation and how well they understand the cultural nuances of the language.

A delightful manga, 'Ōoku' by Fumi Yoshinaga, is set in a castle in ancient Japan. The woman shogun Ienobu ceremoniously enters a private room where lines of men on each side of the room form a path for her. They are bowing down, on their haunches, faces to the floor. The sound of their bowing is written as *shwaaa*. It is a sound you need to experience.

5

Yum, throb, sob

Bodily reverberations

People with a condition called synaesthesia may see colours in response to music, spoken words or other sounds. The chirp of a cricket might be red, the croak of a frog blue. When synaesthetes, as they are known, hear high-frequency sounds they see lighter rather than darker colours. Meanwhile, in 'lexical-gustatory' synaesthesia, spoken words induce a sensation of taste in the mouth. It is possible that we all, to some extent, have traces of synaesthesia. Experts call it 'crossmodal association' ('crossmodal' means using different modes of perception) at a neurological level in the brain.

In 1929, German psychologist Wolfgang Köhler carried out a now famous experiment in which a group of people whose first language was Spanish were shown a set of spiky shapes and a set of rounded shapes. They had to decide which shapes were *baluba* and which were *takete*. People significantly favoured *baluba* for the rounded shapes and *takete* for the spiky shapes. The reason given for this was that there was a synaesthetic crossmodal association of the vowels with shapes.

Other researchers have duplicated the experiment in different ways, using different word pairs, not necessarily relating to recognising dimensions—that is, tasting rather than describing shapes. In 2011 Alberto Gallace, Erica Boschin and Charles Spence carried out an experiment where participants blind-tasted various foods and then rated them according to scales that included real words such as *soft/hard* and *wet/dry* or fictitious pairs such as *kiki/bouba, takete/maluma,* or *riki/lula*).

The participants found certain foods to be significantly more associated with *takete* or with *maluma* than others. For example, salt-and-vinegar-flavoured crisps were rated as being significantly more *takete* than Brie, a smooth creamy cheese. The authors suggest that the associations could be linked to our emotional responses to the texture of the food as well as to taste, roundness being associated with calmness and spikiness with tension. Obviously, if there are foods that are more *bouba* than *kiki,* or more *maluma* than *takete,* then there are important implications for the marketers of food products.

And so with drinks. Correspondences have been found between bitter and sweet tastes and front and back vowels, respectively. Richard Klink showed that 'Bilad'—a fictional lemonade brand name containing a front vowel—was judged to be more bitter than 'Bolad', a brand name with a back vowel. And for some wine lovers, taste 'shapes' from spiky to round can be described using sounds that vary from high to low, such as *flinty, pizzazz, zing* versus *full, unctuous, viscous*.

In our daily lives, however, most of us are unlikely to think of taste in terms of shapes. We tend to express our immediate reactions to good/bad tastes simply by using the conventional words at our disposal. Words and sounds expressing enjoyment tend to feature nasal consonants—*yummy* and *mmm* in English, *miam* (French), ñam ñam (Spanish) and *nam nam* (Swedish). As mentioned in Chapter 3, in English the consonant *m* was found to be associated with pleasant sensations.

If we don't like a taste, we tend to use words with consonants such as *k* or *g*. We hear these sounds in the English *yuck, beurk* (French), ¡puaj (Spanish) and *erk* (Swedish). Non-European languages have different filters, of course. 'Yuck' in Japanese is *fuketsu*, in Czech it's *fuj*, and in Hungarian, *vicc* or *trutyi*. The only constant here is in sounds (*j, k, y*) that are articulated from a place at or near the back of the mouth.

•

The human body itself generates sounds both glorious and unbecoming. At birth *waaaaa* or *waa waa* seems to be universal. Shakespeare gave us a lovely 'tell' sound bite relating to the first of the seven ages of man:

> At first, the infant,
> **Mewling** and **puking** in the nurse's arms.

Our descriptions of bodily noises and movements include many 'tell' words, such as *gulp, gurgle, hiccup, rumble, slap, slurp, snore, thump.* (Again, this is less straightforward in Japanese than in English. The word for a grumbling stomach, *pekopeko,* is more often used by children, but it can also be a cute way to say you're feeling famished.) When it comes to sound mimicry, or 'say' words, we find a lot of reduplication. For example, *glug, glug* and *huff and puff.* One of my favourites is *lub dub,* the sound of a beating heart.

Sometimes the heart is said to throb, and *throb* is also thought to have an imitative origin. The word is expressed in different languages using some common features— the consonants *t, d, p* and *b,* and nasal vowels such as *um, un* and *an*—for example, *ratama-ratama* or *tum tum* (Arabic), *bum-búm* (Hebrew), *dhakdhak* (Hindi), *deg-degan* (Indonesian), *tu tump* (Italian), *tuk-tuk* (Latvian) and *tuk tuk* (Lithuanian).

In Japanese the sound of a small throbbing, *dokidoki*, is most often used to identify a beating heart—typically one that is beating unusually fast or hard. It's often used to signal sexual tension. *Dokidoki-suru* can be used to imply excitement, nervousness, anticipation or embarrassment. Actually, saying *dokidoki-suru* would translate to 'I'm nervous' or 'You make my heart race'.

Suppose you were an astronaut flying into outer space. It is profoundly quiet in space, because there is nothing to carry sound to your ears. So you would become acutely aware of the sounds your body makes, including your heartbeat and the blood swishing through your veins. You might hear *chomp*, *crunch* while you eat, or the grinding of your teeth if you are on edge, or borborygmus, the medical word for the sound of gas passing through the intestine, which is ultimately derived from Ancient Greek's *borborygmós*, clearly onomatopoeic. In Tarok, the language of Central Nigeria, the sound made by a churning stomach is *gùùr-gùùr*—the g sound made in the back of the throat seems to be a given here. A *glop* or a *glug* or *slurp* could accompany swallowing a liquid, while a burp could sound like *gark* if you happened to be Turkish.

Flatulence has given rise to a smorgasbord of 'say' (as opposed to 'tell') sounds, such as *fffffffffff*, which can also be used to mimic blowing on soup, or letting air out of a tyre. But this is really tame for the noise of a fart— although there are many variations in the noise it produces, it must be said. Some attempts to capture the sound include *braaah, brrrrt, phrrrrt* or *prrt*. But in this domain, the prize for sheer inventiveness while mocking sound symbolism in English must go to the Irish writer James Joyce. I am indebted to Professor of English Derek Attridge for his enlightened commentary on the art of onomatopoeia in Joyce's most acclaimed novel, *Ulysses*, published in 1922. He retells how the protagonist Leopold Bloom, after a long lunch, is walking along Dublin's Liffey quays and needs to 'break wind'. He stops in front of a shop window and seizes the occasion of a tram passing by to dampen the sounds of his farts. To accompany Bloom's internal monologue, Joyce gives us a vivid sequence of onomatopoeias of the farts and the tram as follows:

Prrprr . . .

Fff. Oo. Rrpr.

. . . Kran, kran, kran . . . Krandlkrankran . . . Karaaaaaaa

. . . Pprrpffrrppfff . . .

Attridge makes the point that these black marks on the page can only be interpreted as imitating a sound when we already have knowledge of sounds and writing conventions. Knowing that in English doubling the letter *f* does not change its sound—compare *soft* and *off*—we can understand that, by overriding the rules, Joyce is signalling to us that *fff* is an onomatopoeia whose sound lasts for a long time. Another clue that he is overriding the rules about the way we spell onomatopoeic words is that *kr* does not exist in English spelling, but *cr* is very common—crazy!

Here's a hypothetical question: if I had begun this chapter with *ffff, oo, rrpr,* would you have guessed what they were referring to? Or, if your first language was Hungarian, would the idea of a fart appear out of nowhere on reading those three sound words? (It's *pú* in Hungarian.) And for English speakers of today, who have not heard the sound of a 1904 tram, would we be likely to recognise *krandlkrankran* as mimicking it? Possibly, but only if we could conjure up some familiarity, maybe from having seen films of that period. Joyce challenges us by mixing up our 'sonic references'.

Following this principle of mixing up our 'sonic references', Joyce's inventions can be seen as a sort of joke about onomatopoeia, in that they challenge our belief that language is fixed and immutable. Another wonderful example is the noise that Bloom's cat makes: *Mrkrgnao.* To which Bloom replies: *Miaow.*

Because our brains like to predict what is coming next, the deliberate overriding of the normal prediction can be funny. This is the raison d'être of many jokes, such as the perennial 'knock-knock' jokes:

A: Knock, knock.

B: Who's there?

A: Boo.

B: Boo who?

A: Don't cry, I was only joking.

Equally as famous as Leopold Bloom for his farting was the entertainer Joseph Pujol, whose stage name was Le Pétomane, roughly translated as 'The Fartiste'. He was born in France in 1857, and found at an early age that he had a unique talent for varying the pressures in his abdomen. By expelling air, he could make the sounds of musical instruments or of the farmyard, or imitate noises such as cannonfire. His rendition of the 1906 San Francisco earthquake lasted a full five minutes.

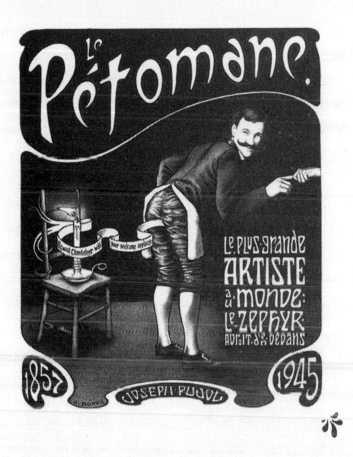

There's not much that's funny about snoring, slob-
bering, slurping, spluttering, belching or puking, but
humans have always invented words to mimic such bodily
noises. I will never forget a made-up French expression I
once heard for vomiting: *faire Raoul* (doing a Raoul). Raoul

is a French given name for a male, but the position of the mouth when saying it . . . enough said. Similarly, among young English-language speakers in the 1960s, the name 'Ralph'—the English version of Raoul—was adopted to mean 'to barf', a word which is itself echoic of vomiting.

Dictionaries and online resources give us lots of lists of 'tell' words, such as for 'to burp'—*oprisping* (Dutch), *roter* (French), *krknout* (Czech)—as well as some 'say' words. A tiny selection of choice 'intercultural' sounds includes *surusuru* (Japanese for the sound of noodles being sucked), *schlürf* (in German, the sound of liquid being drunk) and *glou glou* (French for the same action), while *ikota* in Russian is the sound of a hiccup.

If you are at the movies and making a noise—maybe even making slurping noises while you drink—people are liable to tell you to hush, saying *shh*, or even more emphatically, *shhhh*. The sound is written with several *h*s, but it's really a long fricative sound, which means your airflow is constricted for the length of the word. Some people say *shush*, which is usually spoken in a louder, more authoritative voice, with the emphasis on the voiced vowel sound. Technically *shhh* isn't an iconic onomatopoeic word, because in the cinema situation it doesn't directly imitate the sound of something, like wind blowing through the trees. But it is allied with the drop in volume that goes with whispering.

To convey the same meaning, the French say *chut*, with the *ch* pronounced as *sh* (think *château*) and the pronounced *t* adding a *je ne sais quoi* of sternness. The French word for 'to whisper' is *chuchoter*, closer to an imitation of the sound, as is the more voiced *murmurer*. Many languages feature the *m* sound for this word, with an *s* here and there. A delicious example is the Albanian *shushurimë*, while in Arabic we find *ghamghama*.

Sounds such as these tend to move fluidly along the say–tell continuum. When T.S. Eliot wrote in his 1925 poem 'The Hollow Men', 'This is the way the world ends/ Not with a bang but a whimper', he could just as easily have said 'not with a bang but a *mhmh*'. But it wouldn't have been as memorable. The point here is that 'whimper', although a 'tell' word, is onomatopoeic in itself and brings the rhythm of the phrase to a suitable 'down' at the end. Again, a subtlety for translators to mull over.

Take a word like *swoon*, an old-fashioned literary word meaning 'to faint, or lose consciousness due to an insufficient flow of blood to the brain'. Nowadays it is associated more colloquially with rapture and such a feeling of ecstasy that you feel you might faint. A translator has to take into account the context before choosing an interpretation.

The lady standing on the chair who was afraid of the mouse might fall into a swoon if a handsome knight burst through the door and took her in his arms. The sound of *swoon* in English is indicative of a slow falling into nothingness due to some emotion, unlike the down-to-earth *faint*. Other European languages generally also have 'literary' and informal uses of words. In French there's the 'literary' term *s'evanouir*, 'to faint'. The French everyday expression for 'to swoon' is *tomber dans les pommes* or, literally, 'to fall into the apples'—not necessarily into the arms of a knight.

Swoon is a lexicalised form of onomatopoeia, mimicking the downward spiralling of consciousness, but there is no 'say' word for it. This means that in comics, for example, we are likely to see the result of the swoon, perhaps with a tumbling to the floor, or stars in a bubble, to indicate this loss of consciousness—sound doesn't feature in the scene.

Babies make gurgling and groaning noises, but I've never understood how for the French they could be 'saying' *areuh*, except perhaps that the gargling noise in the throat (an uvular sound) suggests the French pronunciation of the letter *r*. Mostly we first hear *a* sounds, as in *mama* or *baba*, which parents interpret as words and repeat back to the child. In English, some people describe babies' first sounds as 'cooing'. At a stretch, we can say there's a similarity to the sound made by doves, which we also call cooing (and the equally beautiful French word for 'to coo' is *roucouler*). Although they can't make them, babies can distinguish language sounds early. After about 25 weeks they can produce reduplicated babbling—*gna-wa, eled-eled*, and so on. The 'tell' word *babble* itself echoes the *baba* sounds. In German it's *brabbein*; in Portuguese, *balbuciar*; most other European languages are similar, but in Polish it's *gaworzyć*. *Gazouiller* is the word for how French babies babble—and it's also the noise of small birds twittering — while *balbutiement* is the first stuttering attempt at communicating meaning with sounds. During the second year, infants' use of redu-plication takes off at delightful speed until we get to *poo poo* and *wee wee*, or *caca/pipi*.

Which brings us to the different kinds of kissing. Kissing babies softly. A polite peck on one or both cheeks. An air kiss, *mwah*. Lovers kissing lustily—*schlurp, smooch*. Linguistics has its own description of a kiss: it's a 'bilabial lingual ingressive click'. 'Bilabial' means it involves both lips, while 'labial ingressive' describes how we suck air in, due to a pressure drop in the mouth caused by the action of the tongue, and then there is a 'click' with the pop of release with the pressure change. So, next time someone asks you for a bilabial lingual ingressive click, you will know what he/she wants.

In English there aren't a lot of ways to write an imitation of the sound of a kiss. We don't have a click phoneme (a phoneme is the smallest unit of sound in speech that can convey a distinct meaning) as some African languages do, but if you ask a small child to imitate a goldfish in a fishbowl, you will get an approximation of the sound. Maybe Thai speakers were thinking of fish with their word for a kiss, *joop*.

Some comics indicate the noise with *smack*—not a pretty noise. Neither is it in some other languages: *chup* or *jubz* in Thai, *schmatz* in German, and *smask* if you're Norwegian. It's *mats-muts* in Greek, *umma* in Malayalam (spoken in southern India), *chu* in Japanese, *ch-mok* in Russian and *cupp* (pronounced *zoup*) in Hungarian. But across languages the commonalities are the letters *m*, *p* and *b*, which involve pursing the lips, and also the sharp, noisy sound of *ch*, *ts* and *k*, which reveal the sharp air intake or 'click'.

Browsing the net, I found it is possible to download a great range of different types of kissing sounds, such as for 'Wet Kisses', 'Human Kiss' (!), 'Long Squeaky Kiss', 'Long Squeaking Kiss with Lip Smack' and 'Kiss with Squeak'. And for only $2.49 each. Who'd have thought?

6

Cucurrucucú

Sounds natural

I magine the uproar, the hullabaloo, the brouhaha, the cacophony on Noah's Ark—the sheep bleating *baa*, the roosters crowing *cock-a-doodle-do*, the donkeys braying *eeyore*, the doves cooing *coo* . . . or were they? Maybe they were in fact saying *bêê, cocorico, hi han* and *burukk*? Or maybe Noah heard *meh, coo-koo-ri-ko, yi-ah* and *woo woo*— in their ancient forms, of course, the language of the day in that part of the world. Biblical records lead us to believe that in ancient times there was a universal human language (maybe Hebrew or Sumerian). The Bible story says that after humans attempted to build the Tower of Babel, which was supposed to reach heaven, God punished them for their insolence by giving them all different languages so that they couldn't understand each other. Although, the Tower of Babel may have changed the languages we humans speak, it didn't mess with the sound conventions of the rest of the animals.

Animal and nature sounds make up the largest body of documented onomatopoeia. Perhaps this is because animal and nature sounds are the easiest to match in written form, as there is a one-to-one relationship between form and meaning. And so, just as there are 50 ways to leave your lover, so there are as many ways and more of mimicking the sound of a pig in language.

Derek Abbott at the University of Adelaide has documented different sounds for animals in seventeen languages, and a multitude of others can be found on the internet. Here are samples of Abbott's findings:

A rooster 'says' *cock-a-doodle-do* in English, *cocorico* in French, *kukeleku* in Dutch, *chicchirichí* in Italian, *kuckeliku* in Swedish and *kuklooku* in Urdu.

A medium-sized dog 'says' *woof woof* in English, *vov vov* in Danish, *ouah ouah* in French, *vau vau* in Hungarian, *wan wan* in Japanese, and *hauv hauv* in Turkish.

A dove in English 'says' *coo*, in Dutch *roekoe*, in Finnish *kurr*, in French *rou rou*, in German *guru guru*, in Russian *grl-grl*, in Spanish *cucurrucú* and in Swedish it's *oo ho oo ho*.

A duck's *quack quack* in English is *coin coin* in French, *háp háp* in Hungarian and *ga ga* in Japanese.

Oink oink, says the pig in English, *knor knor* in Dutch, *nöff nöff* in Finnish, *groin groin* in French, *hrgu-hrgu* in Russian.

Abbott also lists a range of words that we use to give commands to animals. For example, *shoo* in English, meaning 'go away', is *exo* in German, *kishta* in Greek, *el* in Hebrew, *poshlá* in Portuguese and *defol* in Turkish.

For animal sounds to be meaningful to us as words, they have to be learned, usually in childhood, together with other elements of the context in which they are heard. If you say to me out of the blue, 'Did you know that the Belarusian crested parrot says *rogirogi*?', I will reply, 'Is that so?' and I will immediately forget what you've just told me—unless I am a super-keen ornithologist. The fact that this animal doesn't in fact exist is irrelevant because there are no other contextual clues, such as a picture, that give me a meaning I can understand. If someone mentioned that the Vietnamese grey-shanked douc langur says *cheet cheet*, we would probably only remember it if we had first asked the question: 'What is the submissive sound of the douc langur?' We ask the question because we already know that the animal exists and maybe even what kind of animal it is. It is worth noting that children themselves, even though they copy what they hear, don't designate animal names or sounds; that is done by the adults who teach them the conventions. A three-year-old who has never seen a monkey will say that the noise a monkey makes is *oo-oo-oo-oo a-a-a-a* because that's what the monkey supposedly says in *The Jungle Book* movie. In fact the child is mimicking the adult who makes the monkey noise.

Linguistic researchers Grzegorz Kleparski and Andrzej Łęcki maintain that the similarities in onomatopoeic words among languages are often superficial or limited, and are a result of contact and borrowings. They point out, for example, that the Polish *furkać* or *furczy* ('flutter', from the sound of fluttering wings) was taken from the Ukrainian *furknúty*. A common root also makes some sound words similar, for example, the sound made by a duck—Kleparski and Łęcki say we can assume that it has a common Indo-European ancestor:

> Compare, for example, English and German *quack quack*, Catalan *cuac cuac*, Dutch *kwak kwak*, Croatian *kva kva*, Italian and Portuguese *qua qua*, Norwegian *kvakk-kvakk*, Swedish *kvack kvack*, Spanish *cua cua*, Irish *vāc vāc*, Welsh *cwac cwac* and some equivalents from other non-Indo-European languages such as Hungarian *háp-háp*, Thai *gaab gaab* (with falling tone), Japanese *gaagaa*, Hebrew *ga ga ga*, Estonian *prääks prääks*, Chinese (Mandarin) *gua gua*.

Frogs, like other animals around the world, can sound very different depending on the species (and the time of year). Naturally, the human rendition of their sound is also quite varied. Compare Polish frogs with their *kum kum* or *rech rech* with the Vietnamese *ồm ộp*, the Russian *kva-kva*, the Korean *gaegul,* or the Hungarian *brekeke.*

Some people might maintain that these words couldn't refer to the same sounds produced by the same animal, even given variations with the same species. There is another view, which simply maintains that the 'first language filter' gives us different interpretations of the same sound.

But one constant is that onomatopoeic words for animal noises are full of reduplication. For example, a dog's bark in Russian is *gavgav*; in Korean, *mungmung.* A bee buzzing makes the sound *zoum-zoum* in Greek and *zh-zh-zh* in Russian, while the sound of a rooster crowing is *kikeriki* in German, *chichirichi* in Spanish, and so on. The Australian Yuwaalaraay and Gamilaraay languages have a lot of reduplications for animal names. For instance, 'ibis' is *murrgumurrgu,* while 'grey butcherbird' is *guwaaydjiidjii,* a much more evocative word to the ear than 'butcherbird'. Reduplication suggests that, within individual cultures, speakers use the tools they have at their disposal to make language lively and create enjoyment.

Bigger variances seem to occur in the 'tell' words that are not directly imitating the sounds but rather describing the actions that produce the sounds. They have their own onomatopoeic force. Some 'tell' words like *bray* (*iázik* in Hungarian, *nahiq* in Arabic), *coo, crow, low, cackle,* and so on are not directly imitative sound symbols—that is, a donkey doesn't say 'bray', cattle don't say 'low', a hen doesn't say 'cackle', a frog doesn't say 'croak', but these verbs still carry elements of sound mimicry. A frog *croaks,* a 'tell' verb, but it 'says' *ribbit* or *guā guā* or *brekeke* or *kokak kokaks* or *kvekk kvekk* or *brekeke.* A donkey *brays,* a 'tell' word, but it 'says' *hee haw* or *hi han* or *ii-á* or *aa-ii.* And then there are some 'tell' words that **are** recognisably sound symbolic, like the verb 'to moo' (*meugler* in French, *muczeć* in Polish). And so it goes.

When a 'tell' word for animal sounds is used metaphorically to describe what humans do, it doesn't normally mean that the person actually makes the same sounds as the animal does. For example, we might say that she was *barking* orders to her underlings, but we don't say she went *bow wow.* In the same way, we might say that she was *gabbling* on about something, but we don't say she went *quack.* There's no blanket rule here, of course, and it's open slather for comedic invention. In English we might say a person was *crowing* (metaphorically) about his country's glories; if a French person was doing this, another might try to bring him down a peg by intoning a mocking *cocorico,* which of course is what the rooster (*le coq*) 'says' in French. So a conversation might go:

'French butter is the best in the world.'
'*Cocorico!*'

Bird names provide an extra dimension to this display of mimicry. Some names, such as the *cuckoo*, echo the calls of these birds and are similar across language groups. In Indigenous Australian languages, many bird names, such as *kookaburra*, are said to be onomatopoeic. The bird is said to 'call himself' or 'say his own name'. Researcher John Giacon tells us that in the Australian Yuwaalaraay and Gamilaraay languages, bird names are often a combination of their call, the noise in flight of their wings and a description of both their appearance and their nest structure. For the anglicised word *kookaburra*, Yuwaalaray Gamilaraay has *gugurrgaagaa*, and in two other Aboriginal languages it's *gugubarra* and *gaagum*, respectively. The peaceful dove is *gurugun*, while the crow is *waan*, *waaruu* or *waagaan*, depending on the type of crow.

A wonderful series of apps has been created for different Indigenous Australian language groups, enabling you to see Australian birds, hear their calls and their names spoken in language, and find out more information about the birds.

The languages so far included in the project are Kaytetye, Arrernte (Eastern/Central), Pertame, Anmatyerr, Murrinh-Patha, Mawng and Gun-nartpa. See https://call.batchelor.edu.au/project/getting-in-touch-bird-apps.

What bird produces a whir and a shrill whistle as it takes off? The answer is the crested pigeon. When this pigeon takes off in fright, two feathers, one in each wing—the third feather from the front—produce a whirring sound. The feathers that produce the sound are thinner than the others, and the resulting sound is like a whistle. It acts as a signal of alarm to other pigeons, warning that there might be a predator in the vicinity. Trevor Murray and a team of researchers at the Australian National University made this discovery and ascribed the cause of this vibrating phenomenon to 'aerostatic flutter'. Might this be a tiny version of the whistling sound made by the winged Polish hussars we met in Chapter 2?

The great kiskadee is a noisy aggressive bird found mostly in South America, and many of its names have a Spanish feel. In Argentina and Bolivia it's *benteveo* (well-you-see) probably because they have a black bandit's mask under their eyes, a bright yellow belly, and warm reddish-brown wings. In Colombia, it's *bichofu*é (bug-was), a perfect name for a flycatcher. The English name, kiskadee, comes from the French phrase *qu'est-ce qu'il dit?* (what is he saying?), and although the English name doesn't precisely mimic the bird's call, it echoes its rhythm: a three-syllable call, with the last syllable held for longer than the others. Such names often evolve from interpretations of what people hear; they mimic birds' calls using actual words and rhythms from their own language but with a meaning that changes from one culture to another. And, of course, individual birdcalls vary according to the bird's intention—warning, begging, making contact or attracting mates, or calls made in flight or migration.

Courtship produces the most distinctive and elaborate 'songs'. Some birds, such as the mockingbird, even mimic other birds' calls and other sounds, including phone ringtones and chainsaws. The Australian lyrebird does a perfect imitation of the call of the kookaburra—*kookookookakaka*. There are many explanations for this but the most likely is that when showing his intelligence and survival skills in order to attract a mate, a male bird can add to his prestige by having a wide repertoire of imitations.

As with words that tell us what other animals 'say' (pigs *grunt*, frogs *croak*), descriptions of birdcalls tend to be phonetically based, with often just one syllable symbolising the sound of a call. A bird in English—the Twittersphere notwithstanding—*cheeps*, *chirps* and also *twitters*. It makes similar joyful noises in other Indo-European languages. For example, 'tweet' in Spanish is *pio*; in Polish, *piszczeć*; and in French, *pépier*; 'to chirp' is *csipog* in Hungarian and *tjiep* in Dutch. The common factor here is the high *i*, the sound made by small birds.

In one study, researcher and anthropologist Brent Berlin found that English speakers presented with a list of common bird and fish names in the Peruvian language Huambisa identified bird names because they had a higher acoustic frequency and fish names because they had a lower frequency. In Huambisa, the generic word for bird is *chíngki* and fish is *namák*. Bird names include the clearly onomatopoeic *pitsa* and *tseep*, and fish names, *champerám* and *chúwi*. This result was attributed to the fact that high frequency is associated with quick and rapid motion (birds) while lower frequency is associated with slow smooth movements (fish). (Of course some fish make quick darting movements, while some birds, like the hawk, sail and soar high above us.)

But nuances are infinite. If we say that a bird has a 'song', it is because we attribute to the bird an intention to communicate a message through a call, and because the sound is pleasant to our ears, like music. The same music isn't pleasant to everyone's ears, of course; old folks tend to say that some modern music is just noise. Could it follow that to some ears the moo of a cow is its song, just as we refer to the whale's song? Like the sounds of human breathing, the call of a bird can tell a story. We know that it can alert other birds to danger, signal readiness for breeding, and so on. And birdcalls can be rasping, low, high, pulsating, short, long, squeaky, throaty or simply melodic, depending on the species and the context. We may want to believe that the purpose of twittering is to maintain social cohesion in a general sense, but no one has yet been able to prove absolutely that some types of twittering indicate birds are having joyful fun together.

Some wonderful descriptions of bird and insect sounds in the Amazon forest can be found in David George Haskell's 2017 book *The Songs of Trees*. Two snippets:

The spectacled owl's repeated low, rubbery calls wobble around their crooked axis like a badly aligned tire. A distant tawny screech owl sings a high *to-to-to-to*, an endless, jabbing ellipsis. Insects pulse high drills, clear, sweeping chirps, saws, and tinkles.

And: 'Between the bromeliad's fleshy pineapple-top leaves a frog calls ko-*ko-ko-UP*, a jaunty song.' What sort of frog makes this sound? In Japanese a frog goes *kerokero*. Of course, different species make different croaks. I hear one regularly under my veranda in Sydney, and it goes *bok. bok. bok.* It's a striped marsh frog.

Bioscientist Murray Littlejohn is known in Australia as 'the grandfather of frog recordings'. He began recording frogs in 1954, starting with the Western Australian moaning frog. He also recorded the whooping frog and the hooting frog: *woop woop woop.* His work sparked the interest of American colleagues, who found frogs that conducted conversations and had regional accents. From his field experiments with the Victorian smooth froglet Littlejohn came to the conclusion that *pip pip* was a mating call to females, while *wark wark* was a male-to-male territorial call. The sound of love is light and high, that of threat is dark and deep. Yes to that.

Cultural anthropologist and linguist Galina Kabakova has investigated the depiction of bird and animal sounds in European folklore. She points out that folktales often begin with the introductory words 'at the time when animals spoke', meaning 'at the beginning of time'. Ancient folktales are mostly set in rural areas because that is where most people lived and worked. So the birdcalls most frequently heard in these tales are those that people living in the countryside are likely to be familiar with. And the renditions of these sounds are likely to change when spoken in local languages and dialects, such as Breton, a language spoken in Brittany, a north-western region of France. It is delightful to think that some birds are even considered to be 'speakers of several languages'; in Bulgaria, it's claimed the jay can speak 77 languages, including German and Turkish!

An interesting folk tale is told in Macedonia to explain why the chirping sparrow says v*if vif vif*! The story goes that sparrows were lined up on a bramble and each one claimed to be the king. The falcon swooped and seized several in his claws. Those who were spared started to call *vif vif vif*? (in English, 'alive, alive, alive?') in order to know who was still left on the perch.

In Flanders the cry of the hoopoe is a bad sign for a migrating bird because she cries *huda tut*, which in Russian means 'things are bad here'. And the calls of birds relating to weather events are common. In Ukraine the buzzard says *kan, boże, vody* ('Lord, give us water'), and in Polish the black kite begs *dźdźu dźdźu* ('rain, rain'). The female owl (*la chouette*) in the wild Sologne region of north-central France has different calls in response to the prevailing weather. The folk belief is that the owl has two husbands, each with a different nature, so that when it's fine she calls her nice husband—*côôme* (come), but when the weather is bad her cry is *goyou, goyou*, the name of the nasty husband.

•

The sound of the woodcock to English ears is *peent*; in French it's *pissp*, or a growly *ouort* if it is disturbed and flies up and away. In Russian its name is *barašek*, which means 'lamb', because the tone of its cry is similar to that of a bleating lamb. In Norwegian its cry is *krok krok kvist*; in Swedish, *knort knort knisp*. These are the names of her cattle, because in Scandanavian folk tales the woodcock was originally a young country girl who asked God to be transformed into a bird in order to better look after them.

The woodcock is one of many bird species that migrate from their breeding grounds in northern Europe, the Arctic Circle and Siberia to spend winter in warmer climates in the south, and then fly back to their original habitats. A woodcock's trip might start from Perm in Russia in late November or early December, and she would fly over the Ural Mountains. She might hear *uu-u yy-y*, the sound of the wind in the forests and over the steppes; then in Belarus, *pléščetsja*, ripples on the shores of the lakes, or *plesk*, water cascades in Minsk, its capital city. Then flying across Poland, grey and wet at this time of year, she might hear the sounds of water trickling over the land (*ciurkać*), or frogs saying *rech rech*, or sometimes the approach of a storm (*grzmieć*), or perhaps the *cierp cierp* of a lark, itself on a voyage of migration.

Our woodcock might stop and rest in the Czech Republic, and encounter a brightly coloured bird called the yellowhammer. This bird is known for its song, written as 'a-little-bit-of-bread-and-no-cheese' in English, and *jak to sluníčko pěkně svítí* in Czech, meaning 'see how brightly the sun shines'. Travelling up to 250 kilometres in one night, she flies over Germany, where she might hear the sound of a startled hare, *quietschen*, in the fields of corn.

On a brief stopover in the Alps of Switzerland, she hears the sound of ice moving on a frozen lake: *rumpeln, riss, tropfen*. Then heading towards France, over the Doubs Regional Nature Park, she hears the stamping and whinnying of the native Freiberger horses: *getrappel, wiehiehie.*

It's still cold in France, but as she continues south the temperature becomes less severe. Flying over the French countryside, she hears owls in the woods (*ouh ouh*), chickens and turkeys in the farmyards (*cotcotcodet, glou glou*) and the *clapotement* of waters in the rivers. Thunder (*braoum*) might foretell another storm, with rain (*ploc ploc*) and wind (*wooov*).

From the south of France she might journey over the Pyrenees to reach Spain. Also migrating south are wood pigeons; our woodcock might hear the *bruissement*, the beating of their wings, and perhaps their call, *cucurrucucú*. Now she might follow the coastline to Portugal, accompanied by *tchibum* as waves crash against a sea wall, and the *guinchando* of the gulls.

She might go even further, and fly to North Africa. In either case, after a fattening fill of worms and insects, there's a good chance that she will make the return flight back to the exact place from where she started her incredible journey.

7

Jabber, natter

Poetry, music and metaphor

I chatter over stony ways,
In little sharps and trebles,
I bubble into eddying bays,
I babble on the pebbles.

This is Alfred, Lord Tennyson, writing about a brook. He uses onomatopoeia and conflates it with metaphors —'chatter' and 'babble' are metaphors because they are saying that the noise and movement of the brook is a language. (This used to be called personification, a poetic device that gives human characteristics to non-humans.) People chatter and babble. But to mimic the sound of people's babble we might say 'blah blah blah'. The babbling brook's sound is a continuous stream of noise, but do we hear 'blah blah blah' as the water moves? It's the continuous, albeit senseless, noise that is the feature of this image. Similarly, if we think that both a cat and a car can 'purr' then, when we refer to the **car**'s purring, we are using a metaphor, because we are saying that it is making the sound that is firstly attributed to an animal. The onomatopoeia of *purr* is used in a figurative way to describe the sound of an engine turning over softly and regularly. A feeling of contentedness prevails because we assume that a cat feels content when it is purring. Hence, a contented car engine.

The French poet Paul Verlaine was a master of sound metaphor: *'Les sanglots longs/Des violons'* describes the sound of violins as 'sobbing'. And the repetition of the nasal sounds *an* and *on* makes the effect even more sonorous and full-bodied. This sort of 'sound-and-concept' metaphor is the bread and butter of poets the world over. But it's more common than you would imagine. When Jamie Oliver, the celebrity TV chef, says 'whack it on full heat', he is really speaking metaphorically: we don't actually hit the stove, but the word 'whack' goes with an action and carries a sound of vigour and determination—a bright sound.

A **metaphor** creates something new because it blends together ideas or impressions that are taken from different domains of our experience, without actually stating that X is like Y. For example, we could say, 'You are the sun in my life' (metaphor) or we could say, 'You are like the sun to me'—the latter is a **simile**, meaning that we explicitly say that something is **like** something else, and we use words such as 'like' or 'as'. But we select the bits of the image that we want to compare—when we say, 'You are the sun', we don't normally mean 'You are a nearly perfect sphere of fiery plasma' but rather 'You bring me light and warmth'. Many figures of speech have become so conventionalised that we no longer recognise them as metaphors, such as when we describe something as 'a blanket term'; overused images such as these are called 'dead metaphors'.

So much in metaphor-making depends on how each person sees the properties of any event or object. There is no one way to theorise about metaphor, but a highly favoured theory today is conceptual metaphor theory, which essentially means that metaphors reflect the way we conceptualise the world. Linguists George Lakoff and Mark Johnson introduced this claim in the 1980s, and others have since built on it and also challenged it. Metaphors often carry a judgement of some kind—for example, when we say 'he looks up to her' we are reflecting the higher-order metaphor 'good is up'.

We generally associate loudness with brightness. For example, you could say, 'That colour shrieks', or a designer might say, 'Tone down the volume a bit with the red.' (This illustrates the cognitive metaphor 'intensity of colour is intensity of sound'.) A shrieking colour is a metaphor that also has onomatopoeic force, as do a 'howling wind' and a 'roaring fire', a 'dull pain', a 'thick voice', a 'muddy sound', a 'reedy voice', 'thunderous applause', and so on. In Ireland, a dull day is a 'soft day'.

I have already quoted David George Haskell's vivid descriptions of bird and insect sounds. Here is his glorious description of the sound of heavy rain falling in the Amazon forest; it combines metaphors with some onomatopoeic words:

> An arum leaf, an elongated heart as long as my arm, gives a *took took* with undertones that linger as the surface dissipates its energy. The stiff dinner-plate leaves of a neighboring plant receive the rain with a tight snap, a spatter of metallic sparks.

'The Pied Piper of Hamelin', a poem written by Robert Browning and published in 1842, is based on an ancient German story. A piper appears and promises to rid the town of Hamelin of its plague of rats. To do this he plays a magic tune on his pipe, and:

You heard as if an army muttered;
And the muttering grew to a grumbling;
And the grumbling grew to a mighty rumbling;
And out of the houses the rats came tumbling.

Mutter then *grumble*, *rumble*, *tumble*—the ramping
up of the *umb* sound is deep and threatening.

When we use and invent onomatopoeia we produce language that is vivid and pleasurable. As children we may learn poems by heart and enjoy reciting them, without realising why. I will always remember how, in the poem 'Spring' by the English poet Gerard Manley Hopkins, 'rinse and wring/The ear' describes what the song of the thrush, a small chunky bird, does for us. Our brains are stimulated by poetic rhythms and cadences, along with the repetition of sounds that are meaningful but used in unusual ways. The effects of this are felt in our bodies. The latest research in psycholinguistics (the study of relationships between linguistic behaviour and psychological processes) tells us that, as we speak, we get an understanding of the sounds of our own voice, and of how we make those sounds. Not only the place of articulation, but the breath, pitch, tension and volume contribute to the 'biofeedback' of this information in our bodies. When we say, for example, *eek*, we associate this sound with a degree of tension in our bodies; the local geometry of the mouth—its shape—together with the degree of air pressure and tension in the vocal tract, all reinforce the understanding we have of the correspondence of this sound to its meaning. Further work in neuro-imaging of the brain should add to our knowledge of how this works.

In his 1998 novel, *A Man in Full*, American author Tom Wolfe vividly depicts the sounds inside a prison:

> The ceiling fans went *scrack scrack scraaaacccck-kkkk* . . . Grover Washington's saxophone went *buh buh buh buh bubba boooooooo* . . . *Thra-gooooom!* *Glugluglug,* the roar and sucking noise of toilets flushing . . . and the *tuckatucka-tuckatuckatuckatucka* of spoons rapping on upturned ice cream cups.

We hear the soundscape by way of the reduplicated syllables and vowels and the hard-working consonants—*ck* makes for short sharp sounds, *glug* is a dark throaty sound—while the long, repeated *a* and *o* vowels give us the slow turning of the fan and the resonance of the saxophone.

This takes us back to synaesthesia, discussed in Chapter 5, and the associations between our senses. Charles E. Osgood, a linguist and psychologist, carried out a research study in 1990 with different language groups consisting of Anglo-American, Mexican-Spanish, Navajo and Japanese participants. They were asked to match a selection of pictures with word pairings such as *up/down, noisy/quiet, slow/fast* and *loose/tight* to test visual–verbal synaesthetic associations across languages and cultures. The results were similar across all the language groups. Pictures showing haziness, roundedness and bluntness were associated with the concept 'loose'; pictures showing crookedness were associated with the concept 'noisy'; pictures showing down, horizontal and bluntness were associated with the concept 'slow'. Some verbal examples that follow these connections are a 'fuzzy argument', a 'rattletrap' (a rickety old vehicle) and a 'slump in the market'.

The connections between pictures and concepts also tie in with what we know about vowels and consonants. As we have noted, voiced consonants and low-back vowels are consistently associated with roundness, darkness in colour, low light intensity and slowness (*les sanglots longs*, Verlaine's sobbing violins)—although, in the case of voiced consonants such as *b*, it works only compared to voiceless consonants such as *p*: *blob* versus *blip*. Voiceless consonants and high-front vowels are consistently associated with spikiness, brightness in colour, high light intensity and quickness (the *scintillating* sound of the triangle). Moreover, remember that low-back vowels tend to be linked to big objects, while high vowels and front vowels are linked to small objects (*moose* versus *mite*, *trombone* versus *piccolo*).

Ideophones (concept + sound effect, not generally metaphorical) are sound symbols such as *hoity-toity* that the hearer registers as playful or dramatic. They often have unusual patterns of sound.

One example that resonates is the word *google*. Well before the internet age, google came into being as a misspelling of *googol*, a term invented in the 1930s to name the unfathomably large number 10 to the 100th power (all those zeros!). Later in the twentieth century, it was used as a variation of *goggle-eyed*, meaning eyes that bulge out, in amazement or just naturally. An old music hall song about 'Barney Google, with the goo-goo-googly eyes' comes to mind. But since the launch in 1998 of what is now the most commonly used search engine, the word's former meaning (except in goggles) has faded away and it has even become a verb—'to google' is to search online.

•

A big brass band is in the street going *oompahpah*, or in France, *flon flon*, while the glorious German *Tsching-tarassabumm* is 'oompah and a lot of brass'. Musical sounds are the gift that keeps on giving in the magical world of creative onomatopoeia. Fill in the spaces here: _____ went the trumpet; _____ went the cymbals; _____ went the flute. You can choose from the words *clang, doo-wop, honk, pah-pa-rah, squeak, tluck, toooooooo, waa waa* and *whomp*, or substitute any words that you care to invent. And descriptive words ending with *y*, like *hootenanny* and *honky-tonk*, are a joy in themselves.

If you were listening to an Argentinian tango orchestra, you would hear musical techniques that the musicians describe in specifically onomatopoeic ways. *La yumba* is the accompaniment pattern that is mainly created by bass and piano, although other instruments add to it as well. *La sschumba* describes the ending of a piece, where the double bass and the piano come together in a long, satisfying note (no harsh conson-ants, as in *ker-plonk*!). The violin gives us sounds like *latigo* (whip) and *chicharra* (the sound of a cricket).

On the South American concertina, the bandoneon, there is the *vomito*, which sounds like a vomit and is a crunchy cluster of notes used to highlight particularly dramatic moments.

In Tahiti, you would learn that *'oro'oro* in music refers to a particular, very fast mode of striking the log drum (*tō'ere*) to produce a snoring-like effect (in Tahitian, the word means 'to snore', or 'to gurgle').

Aboriginal people are famous for the instrument widely known as the didgeridoo, a long hollow tube that is wider at one end. The didgeridoo produces an intermittent droning sound that is very hard to make into a word. The story goes that the instrument's name was given to it by white people trying to imitate the sound, *didjiry-du*. They could have tried harder.

We can describe music in terms of colours or other visual effects: *warm, dark, light, bright, dusky, misty, chiaroscuro* (a term from the world of visual art, meaning contrasted light and shadow), *muted, shiny, glittering, sparkling, twinkling, brilliant*. Or textures: *velvety, silken, rich, woolly, jagged, prickly, sharp, smooth, soft*. Other adjectives, such as *ponderous, bold, growling, craggy, shrill*, and so on, can describe a singing voice or the sound of a musical instrument. The choice of words is as vast as the whole world's repertoire of music.

Some aspects of the symbols in written music follow language features that signal long and short notes. For example, a musician beginning to play an instrument learns that *dah* signals a long note value while *de* signals a shorter note, half the length of the *dah* note. So it's *dah de-dah*, which could fit into the intonation pattern of 'keep it up' or 'tone it down'.

❧

A long dash signal is equal to three dots in Morse code. This is an electrical telegraph system that was invented in 1836, before telephones existed, and was used extensively for communication, notably in the Second World War. In this system, electrical pulses represent letters of the alphabet. Operators mimic the sounds of the signals on code transmitters: *dit* for the dots (short sounds) and *dah* for the dashes (long sounds). The high vowel makes *dit* seem shorter and *t* is like a staccato sign. The inventor, Samuel B. Morse, found that the most commonly used letter in the English language is *e*, which is represented in his system by a single dot. Most of us have heard of the international distress signal SOS. Three dots form the letter S and three dashes form the letter O, so this signal is *dit dit dit dah dah dah dit dit dit* (. . . _ _ _ . . .).

What about music and the up/down metaphor concept in the English language? We refer to musical notes as being high or low, with the higher notes being written higher on the score. However, philosopher Roger Scruton notes that not all languages refer to high and low as the two ends of the sound spectrum. In French, for example, the equivalent of 'high' is *aigu*—meaning sharp, pointed, piercing, keen, penetrating, screaming—and the equivalent of 'low' is *grave*, meaning sedate, solemn, important, weighty.

'Playful with a hint of brooding' is how one young music student described the right way to interpret a piece of Beethoven's piano music. Being playful means experimenting, as we saw with James Joyce and the miaow of the cat. In his 1939 novel, *Finnegans Wake*, Joyce invents some miraculous experimental words: *bababadalgharagh takamminarronnkonnbronntonner-ronntuonnthunntrovarr hounawnskawntoohoohoordenenthur-nuk!* is the sound of the thunderclap associated with the fall of Adam and Eve. The word is a combination of words in many languages that relate to thunder. We enjoy this word, as we do other words that Joyce changed for onomatopoeic purposes, because it is not bound by any rules: *endlessnessnessnes, hissss, lugugugubrious*. Joyce would have warmed to Barney Google, with his *goo-goo-googly* eyes. As Derek Attridge says, it is not just the surprising, inventive sound word that we find pleasure in, but also the to and fro between the sound and the meaning.

Another writer famous for inventiveness with language was Lewis Carroll. In 'Jabberwocky':

'Twas brillig, and the slithy toves
Did gyre and gimble in the wabe;
All mimsy were the borogoves,
And the mome raths outgrabe.

This classic nonsense poem, which appeared in the 1871 novel *Through the Looking-Glass, and What Alice Found There*, has a traditional grammar structure, and looks and sounds as if it means something, but the strange words were all invented by Carroll. Sometimes his creations give us clues taken from existing words such as 'Twas' and 'in the'. After hearing the poem, Alice asks Humpty Dumpty what the words mean. These are some of the answers he gives in their conversation: *brillig* 'means four o'clock in the afternoon'; *toves* 'are something like badgers [. . .] something like lizards'; to *gimble* 'is to make holes like a gimlet'; the *wabe* 'is the grass-plot round a sun-dial'; *mimsy* is a mixture of 'flimsy and miserable'; a *borogove* 'is a thin, shabby-looking bird with its feathers sticking out all round'; a *rath* is 'a sort of green pig'; *outgrabing* is 'something between bellowing and whistling, with a kind of sneeze in the middle'.

The patterns of the grammar in this poem allow us to imagine physical forms and actions, so there is a glimpse of meaning, but the sounds are only onomatopoeic if you follow the interpretation above. What I mean is that *outgrabe* can only be a bellowing noise if you accept that a *rath* is a pig. The only sound constant comes from the many rounded sounds that are associated with heaviness. Carroll uses reduplication in invented words such as the *Jubjub*, a flightless but aggressive bird, and the *Tumtum*, a short tree with bright green leaves, and, later in the verse, 'The vorpal blade went snicker-snack!' I say *Yaaaggghhh* to that.

'Translations' of 'Jabberwocky' into many languages abound. One that particularly tickles my fancy is the German version 'Brabbelback', by Lieselotte and Martin Remané:

Es sunnte Gold, und Molch und Lurch
krawallten 'rum im grünen Kreis,

den Flattrings ging es durch und durch,

sie quiepsten wie die Quiekedeis.

This delicious version cannot by any means be a direct translation, but it strives for equivalent wackiness in German. *Molch* and *Lurch* suggest kinds of creatures, perhaps amphibian, and *Krawall* is a riot or racket, suggesting that those creatures are rioting. *Flattrings* seems to be an invention, as is *Quiekedeis,* although *quieken* means 'to squeal or squeak'.

•

Mad magazine is an American satirical magazine that started as a comic book. It has been around for over 60 years, and specialises in lampooning politicians and celebrities. Doug Gilford has created a site (www.madcoversite.com) that contains a historical record of onomatopoeia used in the magazine. Much of it is exuberantly creative. Here are some examples:

arrargh wamp blamp oof yug—a lady and the Hulk making love

blib blib blib-blib—helicopter hovering

bzzzt klik-klik-klik-klik-klik-klik gazownt gazikka— vending machine about to make change *crugazunch*—two cars colliding

dang dang dang dang dang dang dang dang dang—police
or fire siren

dink dink dink dink—tiptoeing

dubba dubba dubba—Tarzan beating his chest

fagrooosh shoossh googloom fush—sounds from a sea shell

ferrip—the King of Spades shuffling a deck of cards

fwop—parachute opening/man bouncing off front end
of car

gishklork—King Kong stepping on somebody

plop phelop—people dropping from the smell of a South
American general's armpits

Reduplication or partial reduplication is frequently at work in these words. As we've seen, reduplication is common in most languages around the world, and notably in baby talk: *ma-ma, poo-poo, pipi, caca, nana, bibi,* and so on.

This is also true of words for the sound of laughter. *Ha ha* is the commonest in English, with variations such as the ironic *har har* (sometimes meaning 'that's not really funny'); the quiet, sheepish *heh heh*; *tee hee*, the impish embarrassed hand-in-front-of-the-mouth; the evil *hehehe* of the bad guy plotting a nasty outcome for someone; and, of course, the signature hearty *ho ho ho* of Santa Claus. Although neat equivalences have been found in many languages, there are always subtleties of meaning. For example, to Turkish ears, *hehehe* or *ehehehe* sounds more polite than *hahaha*, while in Turkish *hihihi* or *kikir* is giggling, and *eki eki* is used for older characters in comics. *Keh keh/kah kah* is for sneaky laughter, and *muhaha* is evil laughter.

❧

'Canned' laughter was invented by sound engineer Charles Douglass in 1953. He created the 'laff box' because he recognised that laughter is contagious and there was a need to 'sweeten' the audience by filling gaps and encouraging them to be jolly. (There is a story that in the Globe Theatre in Shakespeare's time, 'plants' in the audience were used to encourage the people to laugh.) Douglass' pre-recorded laughter machine had 320 laughs. They included belly laughs, chuckles, giggles, boisterous titters, guffaws, shrieks of surprise, *ahhh*s, *oooh*s and even *uh-oh*s.

Text and internet messaging laughter began with *hahaha* and was soon overtaken by *LOL* (laugh out loud), *ROFL* (rolling on the floor laughing), et cetera. Other languages use letter or number symbols to represent laughter. In Thai, the number 5 is pronounced *ha*, so instead of *hahahahaha* they sometimes write *55555*. In French, the symbol is *MDR* (*mort de rire*, meaning 'dying of laughter'). The Japanese write *www* in rōmaji, and it derives from *warai*, the Kanji character for 'laugh'.

Not all languages use the rhyming reduplication that is a feature of English (for example, *hocus pocus, humdrum* or *mumbo-jumbo*), but Russian is one that does: *krestiki-noliki* (crosses and zeroes, that is, tic-tac-toe or noughts and crosses), *plaksa-vaksa* (crybaby), *pravda-krivda* (literally, truth and crookedness, that is, distorted truth) and *ruki-kryuki* (clumsy hands, which online dictionaries translate as 'hand-hooks' but you would probably translate as something like 'having two left hands', which is a bit unfair on left-handed people).

Another form of reduplication particularly common in English is where a single word is paired with another word of similar sound or spelling. These are generally light-hearted and are called ablaut reduplication. A few examples are *chitchat, crisscross, flimflam, mishmash, pitter-patter, tick-tock, wishy-washy, dillydally* and *zigzag*. The pattern is high vowel, then low vowel.

In French, ablaut reduplication often thrives in children's nursery rhymes, as in an old French children's song 'Giroflé

Girofla', or in slang—for example, *pif paf poof,* meaning 'pow pow' or 'bang bang', and *pin-pan,* the sound of a police siren. Japanese has examples such as *kasakoso* (rustle) and *gatagoto* (rattle); and in Chinese *pīlipālā* means 'splashing'.

Arabic onomatopoeic texts are interesting for their cultural content. Haitham K. Al-Zubbaidi analysed onomatopoeia in the poems of Badr Shakir al-Sayyab, who was a pioneer of the Arabic free verse movement. Al-Zubbaidi claims that the Arabic language is rich in expressions that, when pronounced, suggest and imitate their meaning, so there is seldom need for improvisation. For example, in his poem 'Ghareeb un ala al-Khaleej' ('A Stranger at the Gulf'), al-Sayyab is on the shore of the Gulf in Kuwait and recalls images from his home country, Iraq:

> Higher than the high torrents whose foam is **roaring**, than the **clamour**
> A voice that **burst** in the bottom of my grief-stricken soul: Iraq . . .

The sounds he evokes, which I have emphasised in bold, are the Arabic onomatopoeic words *yahdur* (roaring), *dajeej* (clamour) and *tafajjar* (burst or exploded). Then he underscores the idea that all the sounds he heard echo the name of his country, from which he feels estranged:

The wind **cries out** at me: Iraq

The waves **wail** at me: Iraq, Iraq, nothing but Iraq . . .

In Arabic the verbs *tasrukh* (cries out) and *y'awil* (wails or howls) are sound imagery. The poet also speaks of an old lice-picker, a storyteller, as whispering *tuwashwish*, speaking under her breath, to maintain secrecy.

In 'Unshudat ul-Matar' ('The Canticle of the Rain') we find *qah qaha* (guffaw) and the interjection *ha-ha ha*, which is intended to imitate the sound of the blowing wind. Some 'tell' onomatopoeias al-Sayyab uses are *yazqu* (chirp), *tanbah u* (bark or yelp), *khababa* (jogging sound) and *khashkhashat* (crinkle or crackle).

Nowadays on YouTube we can access a satirical show in Arabic called *FadFadeh*, which means 'natter'. It would be wonderful if they could find or produce for us an Arabic version of 'Jabberwocky'—the language resources are all there.

8

Rattle jangle ding-dong

The mechanics of life, bells and whistles

It's 20 February in the year 1909. Filippo Marinetti, poet and author, walks into a cafe in Milan, Italy. He is very agitated because his 'Manifesto of Futurism' has just appeared on the front page of the prestigious French newspaper *Le Figaro*. He asks people at the counter if they have read it and is met with blank stares or lukewarm murmurs—why denigrate everything from the past? He proclaims that the industrial future will sweep away all the cultural traditions of the Western world and that the new Machine Age will bring with it power, danger, energy and fearlessness. And sensational noises.

At that stage his Futurism movement neglected to mention that the newly invented cars were really only available for the wealthy, such as Marinetti himself, but he gathered around him like-minded people—thinkers and artists—who promoted the idea that the progress of technology would change the way we thought about ourselves and the environment, and that this change was necessary. In short, they claimed that whatever propelled humanity forward relied on speed, energy and aggression, and this meant that the old order had to be destroyed.

Luigi Russolo, another member of the Futurist movement, wrote of the noise of modern life in his 1913 article 'The art of noises':

> . . . the rising and falling of pistons, the stridency of mechanical saws, the load jumping of trolleys on their rails [. . .] the different roars of railroad stations, iron foundaries, textile mills, printing houses, power plants and subways.

By this time, Marinetti was attempting to inspire his revolution by creating what he called 'words-in-freedom' poetry that destroyed all established rules of grammar. He used new and random fonts and arrangements of words, and included mathematical and musical symbols. The object was to create a phonetic and visual style of writing that celebrated the breaking down of the established norms in modern life and aimed to demolish the literary and artistic culture that existed in Europe at that time. In 1914 he wrote a book-length poem entitled *Zang Tumb Tumb* (usually referred to as *Zang Tumb Tuuum*). In it he aimed to describe the siege of the Turkish city of Adrianople (now Edirne) during the First Balkan War of 1912–13; he had been working there as a war correspondent. The title derives from mechanical noises: *zang* for the firing of an artillery shell, *tumb* as it explodes upon impact, and *tuuum* for the resulting echo. In 1915, Marinetti was serving in the Italian Armed Forces in front-line trenches on the Alpine front when he produced a picture message in which the typography was intended to represent the *tatatatata* of bullets and the whine of shrapnel, *scrABrrRrraaNNG*. Unsurprisingly, he and the Futurists were accused of glorifying war and celebrating the excitement of its sounds.

Marinetti also gave performances in which he demonstrated the 'clamour of the onomatopoeic artillery'. As his manifesto had proclaimed:

> We declare that the splendour of the world has been
> enriched by a new beauty: the beauty of speed . . .
> a roaring motor car which seems to run on machine-gun
> fire, is more beautiful than the Victory of Samothrace.

He and his followers claimed that the exciting new technologies used in the theatre of war shrank time and distance through their marvellous speed and precision.

A century or so later we know that, except in warfare, sounds that signal modernity are not always harsh and aggressive. Nor are they always glorious. Sounds made by non-humans today include the soft *whir* of the computer, the *ping* of the microwave oven when it is finished, or the *whoosh* of a text message pushing off into the ether. Suppose we were to time-travel Marinetti to a typical European city in the early twenty-first century. In the streets he hears a smorgasbord of unknown machine-made sounds and wonders if Futurism has taken itself in a direction he never imagined—people talk about 'noise pollution'. How could that be? Why don't they all like the noise? Whatever happened to the love of 'deep-chested locomotives whose wheels paw the tracks like the hooves of enormous steel horses bridled by tubing'?

As he listens to the city noises he notices their degrees of hardness and sharpness: the *rat-tat-tat* of a jackhammer, the *clickety-clack* of trains, the *brum-rum-rum* of buses, the *varoom* from a car's exhaust when the driver opens the throttle, the *wee-woo wee-woo* of a passing ambulance, the *ca-tshhh* as a tram pulls to a stop.

And the lesser soundscape is just as new to him. Across the constant rumble of traffic, he hears clearly the *tchak-tchak-tchak* of signals at pedestrian crossings that tell us it's okay to step off the kerb, a gas-powered bus that *haruum*s and an electric car, *prrrrr*. An automatic door doesn't 'clang' and phones don't 'ring' anymore (unless you choose the characteristic sound of a bell as your ringtone). A distinct 'new' sound on the city's footpaths is the *kla-kla-kla* of the wheels on small suitcases being dragged along.

Finally, Marinetti might find himself in a factory, now situated not far from the city centre. He is disappointed **not** to be confronted by loud noises and strong smells. Jumping onto an electric-powered golf cart to tour the factory, he is taken through rooms where softly chattering machines are automatically programmed and the few humans present are glimpsed sitting in front of computers. There may be just a faint hum of air-conditioning in the building. He is so downcast that he demands to be time-travelled back to 1920. So *zap*—back to Milan with you, Marinetti. *Che liberazione!* (Good riddance!)

Another thing the Futurists might have found annoying in our modern world is the ubiquity of advertising and the sensory assault of its slogans. Well before the beginning of the twentieth century, merchants of every sort had been talking the talk of advertising. But nowadays our ears and eyes are targeted constantly: brand names decorate the sides of buses, airwaves never stop telling us what we need to buy. Advertising operates on our fears and desires in many ways, such as by using sounds that resonate with us. Say 'snap, crackle, pop' to most people in the street and they will immediately know that you are referring to a brand of breakfast cereal by mimicking the sound that it makes when you pour milk onto it. Our attention has been well and truly got. Some other well-known advertising catchphrases that exploit sound words include: 'This car has grunt', 'It's got the wow factor' and 'Get more bang for your buck!'.

We may associate the sound *swoosh* with a roller-coaster ride, fast-flowing water or the noise made when someone walks past in a floaty dress. But the word itself designates a particular graphic sign now indelibly associated with a sportswear brand. In 1971 Carolyn Davidson, then a graphic design student, met the challenge to come up with a sign that conveyed motion, looked good on a shoe, and pleased all the Nike company executives. The brand is so strong that the word *swoosh* is rarely translated into other languages when they refer to this powerful image on their sports gear.

Zipper is a wonderful word that sounds like what it does, and can be metaphorised at will thanks to its qualities of speed, sound and functionality (as in, 'I'll just zip off now'). The zipper, or hookless fastener, only became known as such in 1923. Its name was devised by the B.F. Goodrich Company, who first used it in the manufacture of their galoshes 30 years after its invention by Whitcomb L. Judson.

A zipper closing or opening makes a bright or sharp, serrated sound. Even the *z* in the written word itself in

English conjures up a vision of the object. In many languages the word is the same. For the French, though, it's *la fermeture éclair* (lightning fastener). However, in France a zip file in your computer is a *fichier zip*. Even the Académie française—the watchdog of 'proper' French, notorious for its heavy-handed hostility towards borrowed words—can't stare that one down.

Many of the words for 'mechanical' sounds not produced by humans or other animals tend to be metaphorical. Both a person and the brakes on a train can *screech*. The person produces the sound with their vocal system, and this is the primary sense of the word; the term is used metaphorically as a 'tell' word to describe brakes. Likewise, both a cannon and a voice can *boom*, but generally a voice does not *clang*, *ding*, *jangle* or *knock*—unless you are a Modernist or a Futurist poet—although a voice can go 'click'.

In southern Africa there are several languages grouped under the name Khoisan. These languages have a 'click' sound that is considered to be a consonant. In the 1980 movie *The Gods Must Be Crazy*, set in Botswana, the tribe speaks in the real *Ju|'hoansi* dialect of !Kung, one of the Khoisan languages. The exclamation mark in the word *!Kung* indicates a click, as does the vertical bar in *Ju|'hoansi*.

The click consonant exists in other languages in different forms. To get an idea of how this works, imagine the sound used in English to urge on a horse: this is a type of click is called a lateral click. A dental click is the disapproval click in English, and is written as *tsk tsk*.

All words—including onomatopoeic terms—evolve over time; they broaden, narrow or shift their meaning entirely, and often take on metaphorical meanings. For instance, the word *jangle* evolved through many stages until it reached its current meaning, to 'ring a bell sharply'. Originally it was used for birds, and meant 'chatter' or 'babble'. Still later it meant 'speak harshly' or 'grumble', and from this usage developed the meaning 'make a discordant noise', until finally it began to be used to refer to bells.

After this, the jaunty *jingle-jangle* was replicated in form to make *dingle-dangle*, in the usual pattern of the front-back vowels. Like all words, onomatopoeic terms carry with them souvenirs of their travels through time.

•

Bells and whistles is a trope—a phrase that is recurrent, a unit of meaning—and also a metaphor. In English, *bells and whistles* means fancy accessories whose purpose is to attract your attention to a product. Other languages have equivalent meanings for this particular phrase, but they don't generally carry the sound symbolic emphasis, although the splendid German *Schnickschnack* comes close. The Spanish say *florituras*; the French, *tout le tralala*.

The sounds of bells themselves are as varied and diverse as the materials they are made from, the message they are transmitting, and where they are rung. A small bell *tinkles*, but only a large bell can *toll*, a loud, slow, repeated sound; a brass gong *boooooms*; clocks have a velvety *chime*, and so on. These verbs use the typical phonetic characteristics of highness, length or nasality to represent the different sounds. Just as a 'tinkle' is high and jaunty, so is the formation of the word itself influenced by the English production of sound—the position of the tongue and jaw, the openness of the mouth and the roundedness of the lips. Similarly, in the Nigerian language Tarok, a bicycle bell goes *gílánggíláng*, while a church bell goes *goongoóong*. In Hungarian, 'tinkle' is *csilingel*, while 'toll' is *megkondul*. If this resonates for you, then maybe you are on the way to reprogramming your brain to speak in Hungarian!

Railway stations in Japan have long used electric bell signals to communicate with passengers. Traditionally there were four different bell sounds: the approach bell, to force people to pay attention; the arrival bell, which echoes the slowing down of the train as it approaches; the 'act now' bell that signals it's time for passengers to get themselves on the train; and the departure bell, signalling the end of boarding.

Recently, to make the announcements seem less aggressive and to reduce passenger stress, these bell signals have been replaced by melodic chimes. The melodies can be custom-made for a particular station—for example, they can be a short version of a well-known or local song. But all the tunes have the hollow, soothing *dang-clang* of wind chimes.

Some bell sounds can be alarming, or signal bad news. Indeed, the tolling of a bell is commonly associated with death and funerals. But bell sounds can also be a source of great joy—signals of peace, harmony and beauty. In Burma, Thailand, Laos and Cambodia, bells play an essential role in Buddhist cultural ceremonies. Large temple bells, usually made of bronze or tin, are sounded three times after spiritual devotions: *din dan bim bong*. Smaller temple bells with clappers serve as a reminder of the Buddha's compassion: *ting tang*. Bells are used in other aspects of life, particularly in the care of animals. In Burmese, bells called *hka-lauk* are worn by cattle or buffalo: *tong tong tong*. Elephant bells, known in Burma as *chu*, are spherical and their function is to help locate elephants or other animals in the jungle: *ding cling, keng beng*. *Tintinnabulation* means the sound of bells, and covers all of the above noises. Charles Dickens used this word in *Dombey and Sons* (1848) as did the American writer Edgar Allan Poe in his poem *The Bells*, published in 1849. These days it is associated with the music of the great Estonian composer Arvo Pärt. Influencing his music were the sounds of monastery bells and ancient chants that invite meditation. In 1976 Pärt introduced a style of composition he called Tintinnabuli, 'little bells', a music with minimalist harmonies.

What about whistles? In English there doesn't seem to be a similar word to tintinnabulation that covers the sound of whistles generally. The word *whistle* is supposedly based on the sound of a hiss. The passing of air through the lips does suggest an onomatopoeic origin. In the equivalent of this word in many other languages we find the sibilants *s* or *sh* and also the fricative *f*: for example, in Hungarian 'a whistle' is *sip*; in Czech, *piskat*; in Norwegian, *fløyte*; and in Dutch, *fluitje*.

Factory-made whistles, often associated with sports events and training, are small in size but have a high-pitched sound that carries easily across the field. A whistle is the referee's badge of authority, like the star on the chest of the sheriff in cowboy movies. Referees' whistles are advertised as being 'shrill' and as having 'no moving parts', meaning they have no 'pea' or ball in the chamber. There are nuances of sound between those used for different sports, and the force of the air going through the mouthpiece can alter the level of shrillness.

The first official London Police whistle was invented in 1884, by the violinist Joseph Hudson. Before that, London's 'Bobbies' had to rely on a hand rattle to announce their presence to a crowd or stop a wrongdoer, but the London Police were looking for something that was small enough to hold in one hand but carried more sound. The Police Force ran a competition to see who could come up with a replacement. One day Joseph dropped his violin, breaking the bridge and strings. Hearing the sound the instrument made as everything succumbed to the fall, he somehow realised that this two-note dissonance was the perfect sound for the police's purposes. He designed a brass whistle, and added a 'pea' or pellet inside. The pea's interactions with the air vibrations gave it the characteristic 'warbling' sound or trill, and the high decibels it produced meant it could be heard over a mile away. (Pealess whistles don't produce this vibrating sound, but often vary their tones with different shapes of chambers.)

Joseph founded a whistle company that still exists today. His Acme Thunderer, invented in 1884, came to be heard all over the world, in parks and stadiums. Today's Tornado 622 is a bigger whistle with a medium-high pitch, and the powerful Tornado 635 is very loud. Thick metal produces a 'brighter' sound than thin metal, but nowadays plastics allow for a greater range of tones, and the shapes and sizes of the mouthpieces vary the 'chiff'—the breathiness or solidness of the sound.

'Bells and whistles' makes us think the circus has come to town. On the other hand, tornados and thunder produce noises that are rather serious, and I have yet to hear a whistle that says *boom*.

9

Woops, yikes, hmm

Interjections, ejaculations, fillers

Fifteen-year-old Zac is telling his buddies about the time he was recounting a friend's outrageous behaviour to a girl and her father: 'So the dad goes *Wow!* and she's like, *It's lit!*' (For today's non-teens, *lit* describes something that is cool, but most of all fresh and current; it literally happened.)

What to make of this shortspeak? In telling his story Zac uses the verbs *goes* for the father and *is* for the daughter ('she's'). Both verbs are in the present tense for dramatic effect; the story wouldn't pack the same punch if Zac had said, 'He went wow,' or 'She was, like, *It's lit!*'

We often see storytelling like this in what is called the dramatic present. Some might say that using the present tense to communicate past events is a form of laziness, but its goal is to be direct, forthright and energetic. It has the function of both showing and telling at the same time, like the speech bubbles in comics, or the instant-messaging shortcuts of *LOL*, et cetera.

According to traditional grammar, both *wow* and *it's lit* are **interjections**, and are a form of emotional expression.

'Interjection' is a rather loose term, but generally we can say that interjections sit outside other grammatical structures in a sentence, and are frequently onomatopoeic. The 'aha!' phenomenon—the lightbulb moment when everything becomes clear—is a good example that has morphed into a conventional term.

An interjection can be a turn in a turn-taking conversation, as in:

A: Here is the cake I just made.
B: Wow.
A: Looks good, eh?

It's lit, because it's a sentence with a verb, can also be considered an **exclamation**. An exclamation can be an interjection, but it can also be a command, a question, or a statement: 'Stop!', 'Stop?', 'A stop.' It can also be a full sentence: 'What a day I've had!' Like an interjection, it gives us information about the attitude of the speaker, what they want to communicate. To make this even muddier, note that both exclamations and interjections are commonly indicated in written text by an exclamation mark.

Of Zac's two examples, *wow* is the only one where the jaw-dropping shape we make with our mouth corresponds to an emotion—just try saying it through clenched teeth.

More importantly, both exclamations and interjections are considered 'codes', meaning they tell us something about the mental states of the people who say them. As well as telling us about emotions, they can be of the type where we want an action to happen, as in *shoo*! or *ppst*!, or they can mean 'I now know', as in 'aha'.

In literary works, interjections such as *ha ha, ho ho, ouch, phew, yuck* and *zounds* were once called **ejaculations**, which were defined as 'a sudden verbal outburst or inter-jection expressing a strong emotion, surprise, dismay, disbelief, or pain'. The term 'ejaculation' fell out of favour when its ambiguity became more widely appreciated, after the First World War.

There are many instances of this old-fashioned use of the word in Sherlock Holmes novels and stories. For example, in 'The Adventure of Charles Augustus Milverton' (1904): 'As Holmes turned up the lamp the light fell upon a card on the table. He glanced at it, and then, with an ejaculation of disgust, threw it on the floor.' And in 'His Last Bow' (1917): 'In the bedroom he made a rapid cast around and ended by throwing open the window, which appeared to give him some fresh cause for excitement, for he leaned out of it with loud ejaculations of interest and delight.'

Let's accept that a spoken ejaculation is now called an interjection; however, as we saw, some exclamations can be described as interjections, but not all. It may be that one-word interjections are more 'automatic' than what we label as exclamations. Another way to put this is that one-word interjections are closer to a physical gesture in terms of conveying information than exclamations, which are often embedded within sentences. However, if we look at the Holmes example above, we wouldn't write 'with an *interjection* of disgust', but we could write 'with an *exclamation* of disgust'. This is because we don't yet use the term interjection as an alternate synonym for exclamation. But we could say 'with an *aargh* of disgust'. So we are back to the say–tell seesaw.

Interjections such as *hey, whoa* or *yikes* may be directed to or at people and animals. When I say 'whoa' to stop a horse, I simply want the horse to stop; but interjections can also express more complicated structures and contain secondary messages. For example, when I say 'yikes', I could mean 'That's horrible!', 'What a mess', 'Did she really?' or 'I gotta stop doing this'.

Some linguists have sorted interjections into various categories, according to whether they are a 'speech act' directed to an addressee—for example, *tut-tut*—or whether they are expressing mental states, such as *phew*. Of course, to muddle things up, they can be both—depending on the context. Language can be messy.

Swear words like *shit* are actual words that are verbs and/or nouns, but they can also be used as interjections. To illustrate this, as linguist Maruszka Eve Marie Meinard points out, we wouldn't say, *'Table!* They've killed Kenny,' because *table* doesn't express an emotion; *table* could be good or bad, or 'fake', as in 'fake news'. You could be pleased that Kenny has been killed, or astonished, or upset. Because you would not be giving away any information about how you feel by exclaiming 'Table!', your intention would not be to have any effect on the hearer. What's more, it's the short vowels, plosives and fricatives of swear words that pack a punch. Call someone a *moam* as an insult, then compare that to cursing them as a *pok*.

Interjections are frequently onomatopoeic but not all 'say' onomatopoeic words can be lexicalised into 'tell' words. Onomatopoeic interjections like *harrumph*, a 'say' word, can become a 'tell' word: he *'harrumphed'*. In linguistic terms, it has been lexicalised. (This is similar to *bzz*, the sound of a bee, being lexicalised to *buzz* , as in 'the alarm buzzed'.) But not all interjections lend themselves to this flexibility—for example, theoretically 'oh no' can't become 'he *oh-no'd'*, and 'oh, shit' can't become 'he *oh-shitted'*. Let's go back to the 'say/tell' continuum: instances of onomatopoeic interjections sit along this continuum but there is also some flexibility, with some words sitting further towards the 'say' end and some staying close to the 'tell' end. Those in between are able to move around as the creative nature of language allows. In other words, this elasticity allows us the freedom to take the sound *oompah* and turn it into a 'tell' verb: 'The brass band *oompahpahed* its way down the street.' We might choose to say *oompahpahed* because we want to have a certain shortcut impact on the listener or reader. It assumes that the listener is already familiar with *oompah* as a sound symbol. Similarly, a teacher or a parent might have a response to cheekiness such as, 'Don't you *blah blah* me.' For someone learning English as a foreign language, understanding the meaning of these sentences would require a long detour through the sound symbol forest.

❧

The French language doesn't have the same proclivity as English for turning 'say' words into 'tell' words. French ghosts say *hou*, and crowds in theatres and sporting events signal their discontent by shouting *hou* and also now *boo*, although the verb 'to boo' is *huer*. The noise used to frighten someone in French is written *bouh*, and it must be said that the explosiveness of the *b* is satisfying. But to tell us about it you don't just transform it into a verb as you do in English. To translate 'He was booed off the stage' you

have to say the equivalent of 'He left the stage accompanied by the booing (*les huées*) of the audience'.
Another example—an old car or boat in French goes
teuf-teuf, but you wouldn't say it 'teuf-teufed off' as
you might say 'it chuffed away' or 'it tootled off'. I am
ever mindful of the challenges faced by translators.

One of the reasons for this difference could be
that there are three major families of basic verb forms
in French—those that end in *er*, those that end in *ir*,
and those that end in *re*. So to create a verb (lexification) from a word like *tut tut*, the noise of a car horn,
a French speaker would have to choose between
the three categories of verb—do you say the horn a
tut-tuté, a *tut-tuti* or a *tut-tutu*? Too slow, and there
are easier ways to do this—perfectly good verbs like
klaxonner exist, or you can use the equivalent of 'it
went', *il a fait tut tut*.

How we choose our words for their sound value is of
course guided by so many other factors, such as the energy
we want to expend, our age and gender, and how formal or
casual we want to sound. We can play around with levels of
formality/informality at will. *The Economist* is one magazine
that is very adept at plays on words and turning around

the formal/informal polarity in titles and captions using onomatopoeia. For example, in their edition of 10 August 2017, the title of a serious article about rural land rights in Hong Kong is 'Ding-dong'. 'Ding' is a local term for an adult male, and 'ding rights' are accorded to longstanding inhabitants of villages in the New Territories who have privileges and rights over land. These are the subject of dispute and debate, almost a 'ding-dong' battle, an informal metaphorical expression meaning an intense contest where the contestants are evenly matched. (One combatant presumably 'dings' and the other 'dongs'.) Because the author uses the onomatopoeic phrase 'ding-dong', and also delights in the play on words, we pay attention.

A further variable that affects the impact of onomatopoeia is **where** you choose to place the words in a sentence. Think of the sad old nursery rhyme *'Pop Goes the Weasel'* and compare it with the sentence 'The weasel goes *pop*'. A major difference here concerns what linguist Michael Halliday calls 'Given' and 'New' information. Semantically, *pop* at the beginning of the sentence is considered 'Given'—that is, it is not new information. The 'New' is who goes *pop*, namely the weasel. And when we speak or sing this sentence, or a sentence of this type, we tend to stress the last word for emphasis.

Another feature of 'Pop Goes the Weasel' is the tiny pause after the initial *Pop*. This is because the *Pop* is what linguists called 'marked'. Many songs use this for impact. I'm thinking of the 1934 song by James F. Hanley, sung by Judy Garland in *Listen, Darling* (1938): 'Zing [long note . . .] Went the Strings of My Heart' or 'Oops . . . I Did It Again', a song made famous by Britney Spears in 2000.

What about interjections in other languages? Linguist Anna Wierzbicka explains that there are often no equivalents: for example, there is no word for *gee* or *wow* in Polish, and *wow* (spelt *wouah*) is well on the way to replacing *ooh la la* in French. *Phwoah* (said on seeing a sexually attractive person) is like *wow* with enthusiastic breathing plus long-held vowels; it originated in the '80s, probably inspired by the British *cor* and it is inevitably said with eyes wide with appreciation. It rarely needs to be translated, even into languages that already have a fairly entrenched formula for expressing this feeling.

Polish has no equivalent for *yuck*; but its *fu, fe* and *tfu* and likewise the Russian *fu*, the Yiddish *feh*, the Scandinavian *fy* and the German *pfui*—could be linked, loosely speaking, with something like 'disgust' or revulsion. They differ from one another but are equivalent to expressions such as *augh*, *etch* and *pfrr*, and can be accompanied by a wrinkling of the nose and sometimes a baring of teeth. One suggestion is that their origin is in the exhalation of air through the mouth or nose to avoid a bad smell, or in spitting. Both the Polish *tfu* and the Russian *fu* also indicate spitting. Wierzbicka wonders whether *yuck* in English is an imitation of the sound of retching, because it is so far removed from the 'bilabial or labiodental (lips plus teeth) voiceless fricative (or a bilabial plosive), followed by a close vowel' evident in the examples above: in other words, for *yuck* the mouth is open with a back vowel, while for the other expressions of disgust it's all lips, air vibration and teeth. However, French comes quite close to the articulation of *yuck* with *beurk*.

English also has a slang word, spelt *pee-yew* or *pew*, that is used when something smells really bad. This presumably was inspired by the name Pepé Le Pew, a fictional skunk created by Chuck Jones in 1945 for the Warner Bros. Looney Tunes and Merrie Melodies series of cartoons. Pepé is always in search of love, and always rebuffed because of his terrible skunk smell and aggressive manner. The cartoons are written in pseudo-French—*le skunk de pew*.

•

A sound symbol or word whose purpose is, *uh*, to fill a space, or to give the speaker time to pause or to work out how to evade an answer is called a 'filler'. Fillers are sometimes followed by a pause; they tend to be freestanding, that is, not considered part of the 'grammar' of a sentence: 'Maybe you could be more, *um*, polite?' But they are often preceded by a word like 'well' or 'like', as in 'It seems, well, um, a bit awkward'. In some cultures, they involve sucking of teeth or long groans.

In Czech, fillers are called *slovní vata*, meaning 'word cotton/padding', or *parasitické výrazy*, meaning 'parasitic expressions'. The most frequent fillers are *čili* or *takže* (so), *prostě* (simply) and *jako* (like). The French equivalent of the English *um, er, hmm, uh-huh* is the ubiquitous *euh*. It typically follows the French penchant for pursing the lips, and uses a vowel sound we don't find often in spoken English. As with the English equivalents, *euh* can be held and prolonged while you are thinking of what to say. In English, intonation can be used to vary the meaning of some of these expressions—for example, the tone of *hmm?* can be raised at the end to indicate a question or a prompt ('Go on, tell me more')—but this doesn't work with *euh*. While an English-speaking doctor might make *uh-huh* sounds, encouraging you to continue with your list of symptoms, the French doctor is more likely to say just *bon* or *ben*.

A common space filler that is not onomatopoeic is *well*, as in 'Well, I'm not so sure'. In Polish the equivalent is *no*, which can also mean 'yes, exactly'. Learners of Polish beware! In Australia today the word *so* is now used in the same way as *well*. Media reports often begin with *so*.

> Journalist to bystander: 'Can you tell us what you witnessed?'
> Bystander: '*So*, there was a loud noise and people running . . .'

A sentence beginning with '*so*' can indicate that the person is continuing a story where they had left off. It wouldn't have the same effect if the bystander had said, '*Tsk*, there was a lot of noise and people running.'

The Polish *hejze* is an interesting word: according to linguist Anna Wierzbicka, it belongs to the 'urging' group of interjections, and is untranslatable. The word urges the addressee to do something quickly, but adds an element of 'merriment' and implies an invitation to a 'merry action': *Hejie! w górę czasze!* translates as something like '*Hey! Drain your glasses! Come on!*' But the merriment message is missing in 'hey' and 'come on', which could be why she finds it a very hard interjection to translate satisfactorily.

Spoken Yiddish is heavy with onomatopoeic lamentations and curses. *Oy vey* is a common interjection that primarily expresses distress and a feeling of helplessness. But it seems to be a wonderfully flexible expression. Humourist and writer Leo Rosten claims there are 29 emotions that *oy vey* can express, including euphoria, reassurance, and being at the end of one's wits. A handy tool in the toolbox, but another nightmare for translators.

10

Huh?

Lost in translation

There is a point of view that says a translator can choose to be 'visible' or 'invisible'. A visible translator would not attempt to translate an idiomatic Yiddish phrase like *oy vey*. An invisible translator would attempt to pin down all the factors of the context in which it was used, the register, tone, importance in the text, and try to find a way to create fluency in the target language. The dictionary would be of small help, because *oy vey* would probably be given as 'woe is me'—perhaps not so flexible and multipurpose as the original.

The phrase 'lost in translation' means that a lot of cultural and contextual bits have fallen off the language cart during the translation process, and that the flavour of the original has been lost. Sometimes it's easier to 'gloss' onomatopoeia from the first language, meaning to break it down into small units of meaning, and to substitute an explanation or a paraphrase as a way to translate. But a translator who wants to be invisible has to try to keep the rhythms and impact of the original whole text and maybe also its metaphorical uses of words. An example from French: '*Et vlan, passe-moi l'éponge*' appeared originally in a song made famous by French comic actor Fernand Raynaud, but it is now used on its own in other contexts. Translated literally, it means: 'And wham, hand me the sponge.' That reads like an instruction translated from Chinese for an assemble-it-yourself kit. 'Wham' as a translation tries to keep the phonetic intention of the French, but it isn't possible to substitute the phrase that follows without somehow filling in the reader on the meaning-in-context. *Vlan* is an interjection for a sudden brusque action, but has degrees of strength. At its strongest, it can be said to imitate the sound of a sharp sudden blow, as in '*Vlan!* I slapped him across the face'; a softer use indicates a quick response, as in '*Vlan*, I replied straightaway with the opposite'; at its weakest, it is used as a signal that marks a quick decision, as in 'She told us about it, and *vlan*, off we went to see it'. In Raynaud's song the man is naked, hasn't had a wash for eight weeks, is about to take a bath, and asks his wife for the sponge and also for some *guili*, tickling, and *gousi gousi* to go with it. So to translate the whole of Renaud's phrase, with his intention, you would have to resort to an expressive paraphrase like 'Come on, bring it on, Babe'. The humour of the song is based on vulgarity and sexual innuendo and the phrase has been retained in its entirety as a reference in the French culture room.

Humour is especially fragile in translation, and even between people from different countries who speak varieties of the same language. The British are well known for the art of understatement, which plays a large role in British comedy. But non-British speakers of English do not necessarily react in the same way in similar situations, or use the same interjections. For instance, a British comedian like John Cleese might say *oops* on finding that his leg has just been taken off, but I'm not sure if his *oops* would carry the intended comic message to a person from, say, Zimbabwe.

My friend Ruth was born in Australia to Polish parents whose English was more academic than quotidian. She told me how her father would take her to the beach and hold her up in the waves, saying 'Whoops-a-daisy', not realising that this interjection is mostly used when speaking to a child who has fallen over, or an adult who has stumbled and needs help. She herself was too embarrassed to tell him, or maybe she just loved him too much to spoil the moment.

Reduplicated rhyming syllables—in words like *nitty-gritty*, *razzle-dazzle* and *yoohoo*—are a real doozy for translators. Take *hodge-podge*, *honky-tonk* and *hoity-toity*. *Hodge-podge* means a bungling together of different, unrelated items. Unsurprisingly, when I looked for an equivalent light-hearted expression in French I found a lot of words that relate to food; *fatras* (jumble or clutter) or *ramassis* (a heap, bunch or jumble) are closest in meaning. But they didn't have the lumpen heaviness of *hodge-podge*. A *honky-tonk* piano is one that makes hollow and discordant sounds, and is played in a bar-room or saloon (also referred to as a *honky-tonk place*) where pianists have been bashing out loud music for years. Most foreign dictionaries don't attempt to translate this word; a French word for the piano, *bastringue*, comes close, but lacks both the sense of ragtime music and of the Wild West saloon or bar that is associated with honky-tonk. *Hoity-toity* describes a nose-in-the-air snob. It is translated into French as *prétentieux*, and it's *boriosa* in Italian, although there is a multitude of variations depending on the context. But neither word so clearly communicates the nose-in-the-air image suggested by the sound *hoity-toity*.

Suppose you have been asked to translate a text with these sorts of reduplicated words into another language. First you have to ask yourself if there is an equivalent expression in the target language and, if there is, whether it will have the same resonance for readers from a different culture and language background. Then there's the fact that words like *hoity-toity* may perform in one way in the grammar of the first language—they may be a noun, verb, adverb, adjective (as here), interjection or whatever—but this is likely to be different in the target language. A tangled web of confusing threads!

One way to solve the translation problem, of course, is to leave out onomatopoeic words altogether, but this is a solution for the faint-hearted. Translation specialist Helena Casas-Tost made a study of onomatopoeia in seven contemporary novels translated from Chinese into Spanish. She found that in Chinese, onomatopoeic words are predominantly used as adverbs, while in Spanish they tend to be used as nouns or interjections. Among other findings, she discovered that there are fifteen different sounds for laughter in Chinese, whereas Spanish has fewer varieties of laughing onomatopoeia.

She gives an example for the phrase 'my head was buzzing' where onomatopoeia—the sound of buzzing— is absent in the original Chinese text but is **added** in the Spanish translation: *wo naodai weng de yixia.*

Wo—I, me
naodai—colloquial term for head

weng—sound being made (in head)

de—a term to describe severity

yixia—all of a sudden

But the translator into Spanish has introduced onomatopoeia and reduced the Chinese, and the sentence becomes '*Me zumbó la cabeza*', where the verb *zumbó* is the buzzing. *Yixia* ('all of a sudden' in the English translation) is not present in the Spanish either. This is because the final translated sentence would sound more acceptable to a Spanish speaker. Casas-Tost tells us that in her study, 490 onomatopoeias were extracted from the corpus of Chinese texts, but only 82 were found to be translated into Spanish using an onomatopoeic word.

If you know the context and cultural norms of each language you will be a better translator, especially of onomatopoeia. An array of cultural problems occurs when translating any language. One example is translating from English into Swedish, where onomatopoeic words are considered childish and even vulgar.

Most people reading a book in English would prefer it to sound as if it had been written in English, and I imagine this is the same for speakers of Swedish. So if you are translating a book from English into Swedish, and you don't want to seem childish or vulgar, what could you do with words like *huh* or *wham*? If you want to create the illusion that the text was written in Swedish, you have to start from the basis of what the original writer intended: did they mean to be funny, ironic, satirical, and so on. Also, you have to decide how important it is to introduce Swedish readers to the different way words are accepted, all the while respecting the style and register of the English writer.

❧

Many onomatopoeic words are not simply lost in translation, but lost forever. Cultures historically have a tendency to merge, as a result of conquest or preference. As civilisations conquer others or impose their language on other ethnic language groups, parts of the 'conquered' language can disappear. Place names in Australia often have indigenous origins, but were 'interpreted' by the English settlers. For example, the famous beachside suburb of Bondi in Sydney is a derivation of the local Aboriginal word *boondi*, meaning 'noise made by sea wave breaking over rocks'. And the name of the town of Coonamble on the dusty central-western plains of outback New South Wales is a modified version of *gunambil*, meaning 'full of dung' or 'having lots of faeces'. In this case, the Aboriginal people's sense of humour was 'disappeared' by the adoption and adaptation of their word.

Many components of African languages, particularly sound symbolic elements, are no longer used today. Historian and researcher in African languages Lupenga Mphande attributes this in large part to missionaries and their disciples. He labels this 'textual genocide', meaning that cultures who imposed themselves on others suppressed many of the colourful symbolic terms in the established languages. In the 1920s, in their translations of the Christian Bible, missionaries often left out onomatopoeic words, claiming that the language of the Bible had to be 'pure'. Reduplication in the African languages, for example, was ignored in translations, even for emotive meanings. Linguist and translation researcher Selbut R. Longtau, in an article on the Tarok language of Central Nigeria, points out how the translation of the New Testament into Tarok becomes leaden when emotive symbolic words are left out. Also, the lengthening of consonants and vowels—showing emotional meaning—is an essential part of the way emotions are expressed. For example, *kwácálák* means shapeless while *ÁKwácálák*—you Mr. Kwacalak—is the worst form of insult by a bully.

As we saw in Chapter 4, in Japanese manga, text and images work as a single force to tell a story, which gives translators a further dimension to tackle. But because of the international popularity of the genre and its associations with the idea of a social game club, 'non-Japanese manga' have been created in languages other than Japanese. English-language versions are sometimes called *Amerimanga* or *Euromanga*. Their aim is to avoid the pitfalls of manga translated from Japanese, but they have been charged with being pseudo copies of the original manga. However, the theory of interculture—the productive overlapping of two cultures—suggests that intersecting cultures produce new texts. The creators of these texts sometimes do not translate the Japanese onomatopoeia, because they don't have the same resources in the target language, but the reader can follow the action through the artwork/text integration.

Not translating the Japanese onomatopoeia can also add a new resource to a language that doesn't have the richness of onomatopoeia resources found in Japanese. Cathy Sell gives us the example of *MegaTokyo*, an online comic and fiction game inspirated by manga. It began as an overlapping of different cultures and has developed an identity of its own. In this visual interactive game you click on graphics to advance the novel along whichever pathway you choose. But be aware: it's cool, if you belong to the insider group, to know that it's the right-to-left reading direction that takes you there.

11

Slam dunk and the Big Bang

*The United States, life, the universe
and everything*

In the 1964 movie *My Fair Lady* (based on the play *Pygmalion* by George Bernard Shaw), the learned linguist Professor Higgins bemoans the fact that the English don't teach their children to speak 'proper' English. He sings, 'There even are places where English completely disappears. Well, in America, they haven't used it for years!' What would the good professor have made of Americanisms such as *slam dunk* or *bling*?

His worst nightmares would have come true. Higgins and the French Academy—whose stance is also that there is only one 'pure' language—would have had to collaborate to fight the almighty power of American language hegemony. Alas, the French are now happy to say things like *c'est très fun* (it's a lot of fun), or *cliquer sur le bouton* (click on the button). In 'proper' French it would be something like *'appuyer sur la touche'*.

Thanks to Americans, the primary use of the word *tweet* no longer relates to birdcalls. Tweeting by birds in comics used to be shown by notes of music or a word bubble.

Typically, in their twenty-first-century usage *tweet* and *Twitter* remain untranslated in most languages on the i-planet. The traditional birdcalls—in French, for example, *le cui-cui* or *le pépiement*—continue to be heard among the trees. But in cyberspace the universally cool panache of English-language borrowing is invincible.

The television show *The Simpsons* has given us *aaugh, bleh* and *d'oh*. Marvel Comics gave familiar currency to *pow, wallop, shazam*! (Shazam was also the name of the wizard in Captain Marvel comics.) From Batman comics, *throkk* and *wakt* are the sounds of a punch. *Heee yaaaa* yells the Rawhide Kid to scare the horses. The god of the Pokémon world, Arceus, frightens us with *dodogyuuun* (which sounds strangely reminiscent of the *potato-potato-potato-potato* that Harley-Davidson riders use to describe the sound of their bikes idling.)

We can thank Yiddish-speaking immigrants in the north-eastern states of the United States for some juicy enrichments of American English. At the beginning of the twentieth century they brought with them a multitude of words starting with *sch*, which sounded attractive and fun to New Yorkers and were adopted by the non-Jewish population. This sound was a relic of the influence on Yiddish of medieval German, where *sch* is written as a single *s*. The words were often reduplicated, rhyming, ironic and skeptical or sarcastic. Most of all, they were productive, open to play: 'Who said that? Fred? Fred, **Schmed**, what does he know?' Adding *sch* to the beginning of a word is intended to diminish or negate an argument. It can form an interjection, or be added to a verb, a noun or an adjective.

That's a lot for a prefix to achieve, but we should be grateful for the poetry of words like *fancy-schmancy* or to *schlep* around, dragging your feet. A *schlepper* is someone who is tired or messy, and *shtikel* is a little piece. 'Did I see you *schmoozing* with that *schmuck*?' = 'talking about nothing in particular with that jerk?' The *sch* behaviour is a form of phonaestheme and it signals an attitude. Also, because it's flexible, we can invent words like these almost infinitely. Its flexibility accounts in part for its popularity, adding such liveliness to many movies set in New York.

Also originally centred in New York City, *bebop* music is a legendary American creation from the 1940s. (Note the familiar high-vowel/low-vowel pattern of the term. Saying it with the *bop* first—*bopbe*—just doesn't work, does it?) The word is said to mimic the short two-tone staccato phrase that distinguishes this type of music. Just think of Elvis Presley singing Gene Vincent's song 'Be-Bop-a-Lula'. Bebop opened the door to modern improvised jazz and at the same time divided the world of jazz into two factions.

Saxophonist Charlie Parker, in his album *Bird's the Word*, feasts on a banquet of voiced and unvoiced plosives. These repeated *b* and *p* plosives have the effect of a high-energy release, like a wind instrument playing fast and sassy sounds:

> I rock the bebop, the bebop, the bebop
> The bud-bud-a-budda-bidda bebop, bebop,
> somebody don't bopped bopped
> I rock the bebop, the bebop, the bebop
> The bud-bud-a-budda-bidda bebop, bebop,
> somebody don't bopped bopped

Like bebop, *jazz* has become such a distinctive word that it is not translated into other languages, although pronunciations change as the word passes through first-language filters. But although there may be changes to how people pronounce the vowel sound, the final *zz* remains, because that's where the good vibrations happen.

Carl Sandburg was an American poet and writer, and his 1920s Depression-era poem 'Honky Tonk in Cleveland, Ohio' is particularly rich in onomatopoeia.

It's a jazz affair, drum crashes and cornet razzes.
The trombone pony neighs and the tuba
    jackass snorts.
The banjo tickles and titters too awful.

In this poem, the *razz*—an invented word—of the cornet reinforces the buzz, and then Sandburg moves around in a soundscape of animal metaphors. The repetition of the stop consonant *t* for the sound of the banjo mimics the high taut sound of the plucked strings.

A wondrous component of jazz is what is called *scat singing*, which to a large extent mimics the sound qualities of musical instruments. It originated in West Africa, where singers improvised with syllables based on percussion patterns, and in the United States it featured initially in the music of Louis Armstrong, Bessie Smith, Ella Fitzgerald, Cab Calloway and Sarah Vaughan. These artists made solo improvisations on a melody, and their words were onomatopoeic in the sense that they copied tonalities of instruments such as the trumpet or saxophone, as well as the phrasing of the music. One of the most famous was Louis Armstrong's 1926 recording of 'Heebie-Jeebies'.

Different musicians chose different sounds to reflect their personal style. For example, in her scat singing Ella Fitzgerald used a lot of *d, b* and *p* sounds: *doo-pitty-doo-dah,* and *buh buh boo boo bee.* Paul Berliner has compared the scatting styles of Ella Fitzgerald and Sarah Vaughan; he found that Fitzgerald's improvisation mimicked the sounds of the swing-era big bands with which she performed in the 1920s and '30s while Vaughan's mimicked her accompanying bop-era small combos of the 1940s and '50s with lots of *shoo-doo-shoo-bee-ooo-bee.*

Scat singing is alive and well today, performed by artists such as Kurt Elling. In an interview with *The Washington Post,* Elling states that scat improvising is more than just making 'filler' sounds such as *da-douet, da dadi, booboo dup.* He explains that it's the same as playing another musical instrument, so you have to choose whether to make short or long sounds, soft or loud sounds; you have to breathe in the spaces, and interact with other instruments.

Scat singing was also an early feature of *hip-hop* music, which came out of New York City in the 1970s. Originally, hip-hop arose among Afro-Americans who were living in the Bronx, but it soon became a genre that appealed to a much wider audience, and was quickly exported to other countries. *Rap* developed as its musical expression, with rhyme being of prime importance. Here, for example, from The Sugarhill Gang's song 'Rapper's Delight':

> To the rhythm of the boogie, the beat
> A skiddleebebop, we rock, scooby doo
> And guess what, America, we love you

The *b* plosives give us that repetitive outburst so integral to the performance, and then the rhyming of *doo* and *you* brings us down for a soft landing at the end.

The idea of translating *skiddleebebop* into another language seems like attempting to transpose a whole free-wheeling culture. So—although there is little research on the subject—it seems that European musicians have used a kind of 'translanguaging' that has a universal appeal. An example is the French group Caravan Palace, who in 'Star Scat' (2008) give us

> Ke-boppa to the-zip, dang,
> Beep-badeep-dadoo-daah . . .

Here they keep to the *b*, *d* and *p* plosives, pauses, reduplication and energy of the American musicians of this style.

What do we mean by 'translanguage'? It has been around for as long as people have been exposed to more than one language. One only has to think of *le rappeur* (rapper) or *tweeter* (to tweet) in French. My French husband loves to say '*je suis flabbergasté*' (I am flabbergasted), using the resources of his first language to create something new that sounds like what it means. Translanguage is described by linguists as a way of creating expressiveness by moving between a named language, such as English or Japanese, and a spontaneous creation of one's own.

Linguist and educator Eriko Sato claims that sound symbolism is highly suitable for translanguage because it appeals directly to our senses and emotions. One example she gives from her study of translanguage in stories translated from Japanese to English is where the squawking of herons in Japanese—*gyā-gyā*—is rendered as *gyaah-gyaah-gyaah-gyaah* and *gyagya* in two English versions. It could be said that this is simply a more appropriate English spelling of the sound in Japanese. But it works as a sound symbol, which is what counts.

The Sámi people, who live in parts of northern Norway, Sweden, Finland and the Kola Peninsula of Russia, have a form of folk singing called *yoiking*, in a tradition that goes back many centuries. Like scat singing, yoiking is not a 'song' in the traditional sense, but an expression of the essence of something, a bodily reaction to a feeling. The yoik is intended to honour something or someone: you can yoik a friend or the wind with syllables such as *o ne-an o na a na-a* or *li o-no jo no-jo*. Straight from the heart of the cold north.

This indigenous music has not been immune to American influence. The group Adjágas, which formed in 2004, composed their own folksy bluesy yoiks that tell of happiness, the journey of a feather, empty boats, and so on. The band members play several instruments, including a banjo. Amoc is a Sámi rapper from Finland; then there's Niko Valkeapää, who is more electronic, and Mari Boine, whose first release, 'Gula Gula' (translated as 'Hear the Voices of the Foremothers'), added jazz and rock to yoiking.

•

We earth-people have not yet managed to hitchhike through the galaxy in the manner imagined by the futurist novelist

Douglas Adams (whose second novel, published in 1982, was titled *Life, the Universe and Everything*). However, in 1977, NASA sent into space on the robotic probes *Voyager 1* and *Voyager 2* the Golden Record, which had been created to communicate information about our planet to aliens. It included greetings in 55 languages, a twelve-minute montage of sounds on earth, and 90 minutes of music. Whale 'songs' accompanied some of the greetings. Author Ann Druyan compressed into a minute-long segment an hour's recording of the sound of her brain waves as she meditated. She writes that they sounded like a 'string of exploding firecrackers'. Perhaps *pop, shriek, sizzle, snap, crack*? The team who made the record chose to ignore the current scientific understanding that sound couldn't be heard in space because there was nothing to carry the vibrations. However, we have since learnt that there are clouds of gas and dust that are relics of exploded stars, and some of the clouds are dense enough to carry sound-waves; although it would be imperceptible to human ears, because of its very low frequency, sound would nevertheless be created by molecules bumping into each other. Here's the story.

In 2003, astronomers using NASA's Chandra X-ray Observatory detected ripples that indicate soundwaves coming from a supermassive black hole in the Perseus cluster of galaxies. Astrophysicists claim those ripples are the traces of incredibly low-frequency soundwaves, and the pitch of the infrasound note is described as being equivalent to that of B-flat but 57 octaves lower than middle C, which is about a million billion times deeper than the lowest-frequency sound we can hear. It is produced as accelerating material from the brink of the black hole pushes through gas. Scientists talk about the noise as having 'moaned', 'groaned', 'droned' or 'hummed' to itself for 2.5 billion years. That is, of course, if English-speaking ears were to hear it.

What about the *bang* in the so-called Big Bang Theory of the beginning of the universe? (Another theory is the The Big Pop Cosmogenesis Theory—don't ask.)

In 2003 and 2013 Professor John G. Cramer of the University of Washington produced simulations of 'the sound of the Big Bang'. He used data obtained from the Planck satellite mission to observe the cosmic microwave background—'a faint glow in the universe that acts as sort of a fossilized fingerprint of the Big Bang'. The frequencies of the background radiation were scaled up so they could be heard by the human ear. The simulations represent the first 760,000 years of the universe's evolution, and you can listen to them here: faculty.washington.edu/jcramer/BBSound_2003.html and faculty.washington.edu/jcramer/BBSound_2013. html. A bang it is not; more like the sonorous bass vibrations of a pipe organ getting scarily louder and louder and then fading away.

On 14 September 2015 in Louisiana, using the LIGO data collector (Laser Interferometer Gravitational-Wave Observatory, where cosmic data is collected and sifted), scientists detected a strange signal from outer space. It turned out to be the sound of two black holes colliding, spiralling into one another. Scientists had predicted that gravitational waves—signals of pure energy rippling through space— could be heard, and here was the proof. Astrophysicist Janna Levin, author of the book *Black Hole Blues and Other Songs from Outer Space*, describes the sounds made by the 'squeezing and stretching of space'. What is recorded are the vibrations of gravitational waves—she calls them 'the ringing of space time'—which are given as sounds. The sounds get higher in pitch as the black holes speed towards collision, and she describes the final sound of the merging of black holes as a 'chirp'.

A chirp! From the store of sounds that have a meaning for us, we pick out down-to-earth familiar ones and we use them to describe the sounds of the universe. Are we constructing a sort of reassuring reality for ourselves as we contemplate the vast unknown? Will the universe, which began with a bang or a pop, actually end with a chirp?

Epilogue

I have always been amazed and delighted by the vividness of onomatopoeia, but in all the years I studied applied linguistics I found that, on its own, it wasn't considered worthy of 'serious' attention. Yet it is a feature of every language on earth, a direct and uninhibited form of expression. It allows us to be inventive, vivid and compelling, to add colourful new words to our vocabulary. Onomatopoeia forges magical links between our words and our physical senses—sight, hearing, touch and taste—and gives immediacy to the expression of emotions such as fear, joy or curiosity. We use it to describe the world around us, and it can give us clues as to how other people's inner worlds are shaped. We use it to interact with other people and with animals. Some cultures, such as the Japanese, give it a special place, and it makes the world of advertising and branding crackle and pop.

Since the beginning of human civilisation, many languages, especially oral languages, have disappeared as others took centre stage. But sound-to-word mimicry will never be in danger of dying out. We are all copycats, and sound symbolism continues to change and evolve as we imitate other languages and cross-cultural rituals emerge. *Slam dunk*, *tweet* and *ker-ching* are now as well known around the world as the name of the current President of the United States. And the introduction of new technologies and inventions has always challenged us to use words in different ways and to come up with new ones. For example, to say that a drone 'drones' seems to be an open invitation to coin a new word for the noise it makes. Any suggestions?

Acknowledgements

I would like to thank the following people for their personal assistance in bringing this book to life. I am indebted to Richard Walsh for his practical and moral impetus and to my son Philippe, a fiercely loyal supporter who provided the inspiration and guidance for the illustrations. My husband Jean-Louis richly deserves a 'grand merci' for his patience and support.

The following names are in alphabetical order.

Rebecca Allen
Ros Appleby
Michelle Belgiorno
Clara Finlay
John Giacon
Thomas Karolewski
Hiromi Nichimoto
Trish Takahashi

Elizabeth Weiss
Rachael Weiss

Thanks must also go to:
Richard Brennan
Macaulay Hagan
Armelle Lebras-Chopard
Louise McWhinney
Emily-Rose Sarkova

Notes

Chapter 1

Page 4   bwok bwok bekerk . . . Annabel Crabbe, 'Jean-Claude van Damme and chicken impressions: Parliament's bonkers last days', *Sydney Morning Herald*, 5 December 2016.

Page 14   kapow, thunk, wham . . . see bat-fight words at https://batman1960smania.wordpress.com/tag/fight-words/.

Page 14   *om telolet om* . . . Jewel Topsfield, '"Om Telotet Om": How an Indonesian bus horn took the world by storm', *Sydney Morning Herald*, 23 December 2016.

Page 16 signed language . . . Everitt (2015).

Chapter 2

Page 22   'say' and 'tell' sliding continuum . . . Wharton (2003).

Page 28   war cries . . . www.artofmanliness.com/2015/06/08/battle-cries.

Page 28   'harsh tone and hoarse murmur'; 'put their shields' . . . Cornelius Tacitus, *Germania*, C.E. 98.

Page 29   Pakistani cinema . . . Sevea (2017).

Chapter 3

Page 35   shapes of sound imitations . . . Assaneo et al (2011).

Page 36   Ding-Dong et al theories . . . Arika Okrent, '6 early theories about the origin of language', https://mentalfloss.com/article/48631/6-early-theories-about-origin-language.

Page 40   'Slip, slop, slap!' . . . https://www.cancer.org.au >Prevention >Sun safety. Also Daily Mail UK Online, May 2014. http://www.dailymail. co.uk/news/article-2635981

Page 42   'tlot-tlot' . . . https://www.poets.org/poetsorg/poem/highway-man. Note that the last three lines cited here are repeated from the first stanza.

Page 43   nasal sounds . . . see www.quora.com/What-are-some-of-the-most-nasal-languages-in-the-world.

Page 44   nasal sounds . . . Crystal (2011), p. 321; *mellifluous* . . . Crystal (2007) p. 168 and 170.

Page 45   'sn' beginning words . . . Philps (2011).

Page 46   *klump* . . . Carling and Johansson (2014).

Chapter 4

Page 57   *kirakira* . . . Caldwell (2010).

Page 58   *noronoro* . . . Nicolae (2014).

Page 63   *shiiiin* . . . Sharlin (2010).

Page 64   ohohoho . . . Sell (2011).

Page 65   *kojinmari* . . . Inose (2017).

Page 65   Yoshinaga's manga series . . . en.wikipedia.org/wiki/Ōoku:_The_ Inner_Chambers.

Chapter 5

Page 70   *kiki/bouba* . . . Gallace, Boschin and Spence (2011), p. 38.

Pages 70–1   'Bilad'/'Bolad' . . . Klink (2000).

Page 72   'Mewling and puking' . . . from a monologue in Shakespeare's *As You Like It*, Act II, Scene VII. The speech compares the seven stages of Man's life.

Chapter 6

Page 88   cock-a-doodle-do . . . Derek Abbott, see: www.eleceng.adelaide. edu.au/Personal/dabbott/animal.html. See also Gary Nunn, 'Animal noises in different languages', *The Guardian*, 17 November 2014.

Page 90   the sound made by a duck . . . Kleparski and Łęcki (2002), p.10/14.

Page 91   Yuwaalaraay and Gamilaraay languages . . . Giacon (2013), p. 259.

Page 93   Yuwaalaray and Gamilaraay languages . . . see htpp//yuwaalarayy. org.

Page 94   whir and a shrill whistle . . . Murray et al (2017).

Page 96   *pitsa* and *champerám* . . . Berlin (1994).

Page 98   to-to-to-to . . . Haskell (2017), p. 20.

Page 98   ko-ko-UP . . . Haskell (2017), p. 8.

Chapter 7

Page 105   'chatter over stony ways' . . . from Alfred, Lord Tennyson, 'The
            Brook: An Idyl' (1833).

Page 106   '*Les sanglots longs/Des violons*' from Verlaine's 'Chanson
            d'automne', *Poèmes Saturniens* (1866).

Page 107   good is up . . . Lakoff and Johnson (1980), p.37 Note that con-
            ceptual metaphors are written in upper case, but I have not followed
            this convention in the text here. See also Barbara Lasserre (2009)
            'Metaphor and the Design Critique', thesis, Masters of Education
            Honours, University of Technology Sydney, Sydney.

Page 108   *took took* . . . Haskell (2017), p. 6.

Page 110   '*scrack scrack scraaaacccckkkkk*' . . . Wolfe (1998), pp. 329 and
            385.

Page 111   noisy/quiet, slow/fast, loose/tight . . . Osgood (1990), pp. 116,
            305.

Page 116   *aigu/grave* . . . Scruton (1997), p. 21.

Page 116   'playful with a hint of brooding' . . . Woolfe (2006); see also
            crosseyedpianist.com.

Page 117–18 *brillig* means . . . from Lewis Carroll's *Through the Looking
            Glass* (iBooks, 1991, pp. 153–6).

Page 118   'Brabbelback' . . . www76.pair.com/keithlim/jabberwocky/
            translations/german2.html.

Page 121   Turkish laughter . . . forum.wordreference.com/threads/
            laughter-hahahehe.419591.

Page 123   Arabic poetry . . . Al-Zubbaidi (2014).

Chapter 8

Pages 127, 130   Futurist Manifesto . . . see http://viola.informatik.uni-
            bremen.de/typo/fileadmin/media/lernen/Futurist_Manifesto.pdf

Page 128   Russolo (1913), p. 7. See also Luigi Russolo (1997) 'The Art of
            Noises' in *Die Wiener Gruppe: A moment of modernity 1954-1960 /
            The visual works and the actions*, ed Peter Weibel, SpringerWien New

York, La Biennale di Venezia 1997, available from: http://www.ubu. com/papers/russolo.html.

Page 129   'The Winged Victory of Samothrace' is a famous and graceful second century Greek sculpture of Nike, the Greek goddess of Victory.

Page 132   the Nike 'swoosh' . . . creativemarket.com/blog/the-35-nike-logo-and-thewoman-who-designed-it.

Chapter 9

Page 147   '*Table!* They've killed Kenny' . . . Meinard (2015), p. 154.

Page 150   'Given' and 'New' . . . Halliday (1985), p. 277.

Page 155   *hejże* . . . Wierzbicka, (2001), p. 298–9

Page 155   *oy vey* . . . Rosten (1968), p. 115.

Page 163   *wo naodai weng de yixia* . . . Casas-Tost (2014), p. 44.

Page 166   'textual genocide' . . . Mphande (1992), p.119.

Chapter 11

Page 176   making filler sounds . . . Jess Righthand, 'Elling takes the gibberish out of scat', *The Washington Post*, 28 October 2011.

Page 178   translanguage . . . Sato (2017).

Page 180   Ann Druyan . . . see https://voyager.jpl.nasa.gov/golden-record/.

Page 180   sound in outer space . . . https://gizmodo.com/there-actually-is-sound-in-outer-space-1738420340.

Page 182   'squeezing and stretching of space'; 'the ringing of space time' . . . Levin (2016), loc. 50 of 3631.

Page 182   'chirp' . . . Levin (2016), loc. 2553 of 3631.

Bibliography

Abelin, Åsa (2015) 'Phonaesthemes and sound symbolism in Swedish brand names', *Ampersand*, vol. 2, pp. 19–29.

Al-Zubbaidi, H.K. (2014) 'The functions of onomatopoeia in Modern English and Arabic poetry: A study in selected poems by Lawrence and al-Sayyab', *Advances in Language and Literary Studies*, vol. 5, no. 6, pp. 181–93.

Assaneo, M. F., et al. (2011) 'The anatomy of onomatopoeia', *PLOS ONE*, vol. 6, no. 12, e28317.

Athaide, G.A. & Klink, R.R. (2012) 'Creating global brand names: The use of sound symbolism', *Journal of Global Marketing*, vol. 25, pp. 202–12.

Attridge, D. (1984) 'Language as imitation: Jakobson, Joyce, and the art of onomatopoeia', *Comparative Literature*, vol. 99, no. 5, pp. 1116–40.

Bankieris, K. & Simner, J. (2013) 'Sound symbolism in synesthesia: Evidence from a lexical–gustatory synesthete', *Neurocase*, vol. 20, no. 6, pp. 640–51.

Berlin, B. (1994) 'Evidence for pervasive synthetic sound symbolism in ethnozoological nomenclature', in L. Hinton, J. Nichols & J.J. Ohala (eds), *Sound Symbolism*, Cambridge University Press, New York, pp. 76–93.

Berliner, P. (1994) *Thinking in Jazz: The infinite art of improvisation*, University of Chicago Press, Chicago.

Cabrera, J.C.M. (2016) 'Onomatopoeia and the meaningful interpretation of bird calls', in M.A. Flaksman & O.I. Brodovich (eds), *Phonosemantics. In commemoration of Professor Dr Stanislav Voronin's 80th anniversary*, ANCO University of Education Districts, St Petersburg, pp. 73–8.

Caldwell, J. (2010) 'Iconic semantics in phonology: A corpus study of Japanese mimetics', thesis for Master of Arts, Brigham Young University, Utah. Retrieved 18/02/2018 from www.researchgate.net/publication/268013425.

Carling, G. & Johansson, N. (2014) 'Motivated language change', *Acta Linguistica Hafniensia*, vol. 46, no. 2, pp. 199–217.

Casas-Tost, H. (2014) 'Translating onomatopoeia from Chinese into Spanish: A corpus-based analysis', *Perspectives: Studies in Translatology*, vol. 22, no. 1, pp. 39–55.

Conan Doyle, Sir Arthur (1904) *Sherlock Holmes: The Dark Mysteries*, online, Guttenberg library.

Crystal, D. (2007) *Words Words Words*, Oxford University Press, New York.

—— (2011) *Dictionary of Linguistics and Phonetics*, 6th edn, John Wiley & Sons Inc., ProQuest Ebook Central. Retrieved 13/07/2018.

Druyan, A. & Sagan, Carl, (1978) *Murmurs of Earth: The Voyager Interstellar Record*, Random House, New York.

Everitt, A. (2015) 'Baaaa: Developing an understanding of Onomatopoeia through New Zealand Sign Language'. Retrieved 20/05/2018 from www.academia.edu/21145432/

Fukada, H. (2003) *Jazz Up Your Japanese with Onomatopoeia*, translated by T. Gally, Kodansha International, New York.

Gallace, A., Boschin, E. & Spence, C. (2011) 'On the taste of "Bouba" and "Kiki": An exploration of word–food associations in neurologically normal participants', *Cognitive Neuroscience*, vol. 2, no. 1, pp. 34–46.

Giacon, J. (2013) 'Etymology of Yuwaalaraay Gamilaraay bird names', in R. Mailhammer (ed.), *Lexical and Structural Etymology*, de Gruyter Mouton, Boston, p. 251.

Goscinny, R. & Uderzo, A. (1965) *Astérix the Gaul*, translated by Anthea Bell and Derek Hockridge, Dargaud, Paris.

Haskell, D.G. (2017) *The Songs of Trees: Stories from nature's great connectors*, Black Inc., Melbourne.

Halliday, M.A.K. (1985) *An Introduction to Functional Grammar*, Edward Arnold, London.

Inose, H. (2017) *Translating Japanese Onomatopoeia and Mimetic Words*. Retrieved 08/07/2017 from www.academia.edu/1448796, p. 97.

Kabakova, G. (2017) '"J' serons pris! J' serons pris" chante la brouette: Les "mimologismes" dans le folklore européen', in *Verba sonandi: Étude de la représentation linguistique des cris d'animaux*, E. Rakhilina, J.-M. Merle,

I. Kor-Chahine (eds), Presses Universitaires de Provence (PUP), Aix-en-Provence, pp. 299–308.

Kagitani, T. et al. (2014) 'Sound symbolic relationship between onomatopoeia and emotional evaluations in taste', *Proceedings of the 36th Annual Cognitive Science Society Meeting* (CogSci2014).

Kleparski, G.A. & Lecki, A.M. (2002) *Dash, splash and hush: Arbitrariness versus onomatopoeia, The traditional approach to sound symbolism: A review*, Zeszyty Naukowe Uniwersytetu Rzeszowskiego, Seria Filologiczna, Zeszyt, Studia Anglica Resoviensia 1, vol. 6, Lublin.

Klink, R.R. (2000) 'Creating brand names with meaning: The use of sound symbolism', *Marketing Letters*, vol. 11, no. 1, pp. 5–20.

Lakoff, G. & Johnson, M. (1980) *Metaphors We Live By*, University of Chicago Press, Chicago.

Leonardi, F.M. (2015) *Phonesthemes in Latin Language*. Retrieved 12/11/2017 from www.academia.edu/17549917/Phonesthemes_in_Latin_Language.

Levin, J. (2016) *Black Hole Blues and Other Songs From Outer Space*, The Bodley Head, London.

Longtau, S. (2016) 'Explorations of sound symbolism and meaning in the Tarok orthography and translation', *JOLAN: Journal of the Linguistic Association of Nigeria*, vol. 2, pp. 1–16.

McKay, B. & McKay, K. (2015) *The Art of Manliness*. Retrieved 06/07/2017 from https://www.artofmanliness.com/articles/battle-cries/

Manea, P. (2017) 'Melodic refrains in Japanese train stations: The management of passenger behaviour through the use of electric bells', in C. Guillebaud (ed.), *Towards an Anthropology of Ambient Sound*, Routledge, New York, p. 108.

Meinard, M.E.M. (2015) 'Distinguishing onomatopoeia from interjections', *Journal of Pragmatics*, vol. 76, pp. 150–68.

Mphande, L. (1992) 'Ideophones and African verse', *Research in African Literatures*, vol. 23, pp. 117–29.

Müller, A. (2016) 'What are some of the most nasal languages in the world?' Retrieved 06/08/2017 from www.quora.com/What-are-some-of-the-most-nasal-languages-in-the-world.

Murray, T., Zeil, J. & Magrath, R.D. (2017) 'Sounds of modified flight feathers reliably signal danger in a pigeon', *Current Biology*, vol. 27, no. 22, pp. 3520–5.

Nicolae, R. (2014) 'Musicality and onomatopoeia use in Miyazawa Kenji's short stories', *Linguistic and Philosophical Investigations*, vol. 13, pp. 297–313.

Nunn, G. (2014) 'Animal noises in different languages', *The Guardian*, 17 November.

Ohala, J.J. (1994) 'The frequency code underlies the sound-symbolic use of voice pitch', in L. Hinton, J. Nichols & J.J. Ohala (eds), *Sound Symbolism*, Cambridge University Press, Cambridge, pp. 325–47. Retrieved 10/11/2017 from linguistics.berkeley.edu/~ohala/papers/freq_code.pdf.

Osgood, C. (1990) 'The cross-cultural generality of visual-verbal synesthetic tendencies', in C.E. Osgood & C.S. Tzeng (eds), *Language, Meaning, and Culture: The selected papers of C.E. Osgood*, Praeger, New York, pp. 146–69.

Oszmianska, A. (2001) 'Sound symbolism as a universal drive to associate sound with meaning: A comparison between English and Japanese', *Poznan Studies in Contemporary Linguistics*, vol. 37, pp. 147–55.

Philps, D. (2011) 'Reconsidering phonæsthemes: Submorphemic invariance in English "sn- words"', *Lingua*, vol. 121, no. 6, pp. 1121–37.

Ramachandran, V.S. & Hubbard, E.M. (2001) 'Synaesthesia—a window into perception, thought and language', *Journal of Consciousness Studies*, vol. 8, no. 12, pp. 3–34.

Rosten, L. (1968) *The Joys of Yiddish*, McGraw-Hill, New York.

Russolo, L. (2015) *Luigi Russolo, The Art of Noises, futurist manifesto*, 1913, (trans. Robert Filliou, 1967), UbuClassics, New York.

Sasamoto, R. (2015) 'Onomatopoeia and argumentation in Japanese manga. The role of images in persuasive communication', paper delivered at 14th International Pragmatics Association Conference.

Sasamoto, R. & Jackson, R. (2016) 'Onomatopoeia—showing-word or saying-word? Relevance theory, lexis, and the communication of impressions', *Lingua*, vol. 175, pp. 36–53.

Sato, E. (2017) 'Translanguaging in translation: Evidence from Japanese mimetics', *International Journal of Linguistics and Communication*, vol. 5, no. 1, pp. 11–26.

Scruton, R. (1997) *The Aesthetics of Music*, Oxford University Press, Oxford.

Sell, C. (2011) 'Manga translations and interculture', *Mechademia*, vol. 6, pp. 93–108.

Sevea, I. (2017) *'Kharaak Kita Oi': Masculinity Caste and Gender in Punjabi Films*. Retrieved 12/12/2017 from www.academia.edu/8272267.

Sharlin, N. (2010) *Sounds Like . . . Understanding Japanese Sound Symbolism*. Retrieved 03/01/2018 from https://www.swarthmore.edu/sites/default/files/assets/documents/linguistics/2010_NaomiSharlin.pdf

Stewart, M.L. (1987) 'Stylistic environment and the scat singing styles of Ella Fitzgerald and Sarah Vaughan', *Jazzforschung/Jazz Research*, vol. 19, pp. 61–76.

Stone, A. (2010) 'Ka-Pow! Using ASL and English to explore narratives in comics', thesis for Master of Arts, University of California, San Diego. Retrieved 06/02/2018 from www.researchgate.net/publication/235611666.

Tacitus, C. (2013) *The Germany and the Agricola of Tacitus*, The Oxford Translation Revised, Project Gutenberg ebook. Retrieved 7/12/2017 from www.gutenberg.org/ebooks/7524

Toratani, K. (2005) 'A cognitive approach to mimetic aspect in Japanese', *Proceedings of the Annual Meeting of the Berkeley Linguistics Society*, vol. 31, no. 1, pp. 335–46.

Wajnryb, R. (2006) *Australian Place Name Stories*, Lothian Books, Melbourne, p. 23.

Ward, J. & Simner, J. (2003) 'Lexical-gustatory synaesthesia: Linguistic and conceptual factors', *Cognition*, vol. 89, pp. 237–61.

Wharton, T. (2003) 'Interjections, language, and the "showing"/"saying" continuum', *Pragmatics and Cognition*, vol. 11, no. 1, pp. 39–91.

Wierzbicka, A. (1992) 'The semantics of interjection', *Journal of Pragmatics*, vol. 18, pp. 159–92.

—— (2001) *Cross-Cultural Pragmatics*, 2nd edn, Mouton de Gruyter, Berlin.

Wolfe, T. (1998), *A Man in Full*, The Dial Press, New York.

Woolfe, J. (2006) 'A musician's English: The challenge awaiting international students in tertiary music programs in Australia', *TESOL in Context*, vol. 16, no. 1, pp. 18–25.

Yoshinaga, F., 'Ōoku: The Inner Chambers'. Retrieved 12/01/2018 from https://en.wikipedia.org/wiki/Ōoku:_The_Inner_Chambers.